Coro

Coro

Creation, Concepts, Connections

A BOOK
ABOUT THE FOUNDERS,
THEIR IDEAS,
AND HOW THEIR IDEAS
BECAME REALITIES

Fran Aleshire
Editor

Coro National Alumni Association

This book is dedicated to
Van Duyn Dodge
and
W. Donald Fletcher
Coro's Founders

Acknowledgements

This book was conceived by charter members of the Coro National Alumni Association to honor the founders of Coro at the time of the 50th Anniversary of Coro in 1992. Members were concerned that no chronicle of the research period or the early days of the Foundation existed. There was concern that many of the original documents and early memories were fading. This was considered a particular loss since Coro's educational research is not only of interest to those who participated in the progam, but the unique nature of Coro's approach makes these findings of general interest to educators and those interested in developing community leadership and commitment from citizens. Fran Aleshire volunteered to begin tape recording the recollections of the pioneers and to act as editor; other CNAA members came foreward with photos, documents and encouragement. Staff members from the early days were especially helpful.

Here is our special opportunity to recognize those individuals without whom this project would not have been completed. Uri Manheim provided the consistent sparkplug for the project; he just wouldn't give up in spite of all the difficulties. Ray Roeder, the first president of the CNAA, was the crisis manager who moved us along when all else failed. Jerry Jones was chief archivist; he searched the San Francisco office for photos and clippings and provided key information. Ben Neufeld

conducted many interviews in Los Angeles. Ruth James, who is working on cataloguing the Fletcher papers, helped fill in some gaps. Jim Schoning, David Sibbet and John Greenwood spent hours with the editor, providing her with anecdotes and insights about Coro concepts and methodology.

Austin Woodward wrote the L.A. chapter; Karin Eisele and Kenneth Mountcastle contributed the New York account, and Don Kornblet and Robert Eilermann, Jr. collaborated on the St. Louis piece. Frank Aleshire, Austin Woodward and Amos White critiqued and proofed. Tom Hoeber gave valuable publishing advice. Carol Tharp filled in many blanks, and Ed Gerber organized the resources of the CNAA. Then David Sibbet made a major contribution when he stepped in to take charge of formatting, final editing, graphics and publishing. So this book is the effort of many minds and much dedication, all out of gratitude to Coro and its founders. Beyond those mentioned, there were many more who helped and who are quoted in the text.

Following is a list of contributors from Coro, other than those already mentioned: David Abel, Bob Coate, Ralph Cole, James Conn, Bruce Corwin, Helen DeWar, Lowell Dodge, Tom Dooley, Drew Dougherty, Alan E. Ellis, Assemblyman Vic Fazio, Senator Diane Feinstein, Marlene Garcia, Libby Gatov, Michael Giger, John Johnson, Maria Nicholas Kelly, Joanne Kozberg, Krist

Lane, Assemblyman Jerry Lewis, Don Livingston, Tom McFletcher, John Mockler, Marion Pulsifer, John Robinson, Sam Sewall, Gene Siskel, Fred Taugher, Bill Whiteside.

Friends of Coro who are quoted are: Thornton Bradshaw, T.A. Brooks, George Cameron, John Cushing, Daniel DeCarlo, Lloyd Dennis, Donald Ehrman, John W. Hanley, Preston Hotchkis, President John F. Kennedy, Richard Lyman, Chester R. MacPhee, Lloyd McBride, William Pemberton, President Ronald Reagan, Michael Roos, John Witter.

Contents

CHRONOLOGY, EXPANSION AND CHANGES

ACHIEVEMENTS

VISIONS OF THE FUTURE

Introduction

"No sooner do you set foot on American soil than you find yourself in a sort of tumult; a confused clamor rises on every side, and a thousand voices are heard at once, each expressing some social requirement." In the mid-1800's, Alexis de Tocqueville, who was probably the keenest observer of the tendencies of democracy in America, penned these words. He also anticipated the popularity of today's talk radio when he wrote: "To take a hand in the government of society and to talk about it is his (the citizen's) most important business and the greatest pleasure he knows . . . an American does not know how to converse, but he argues; he does not talk, he expatiates."

The intense interest Americans are taking in "restructuring" their government is not a new phenomenon. Our efforts to re-create ourselves has been a preoccupation over the several centuries of our civic life. When we feel awash in change, we may feel this ferment and chronic dissatisfaction is a negative, but we also know, in our hearts, that the fascination of Americans for what's happening in their democracy and the energy they bring to trying to make things better is also our greatest strength and promise.

This book is about several Americans who took a hard look at their country's way of governing just after the trauma of World War II. They thought we could and must do better. They decided to conduct fresh, original research, and agreed that educating youth would pro-

duce the most long-lasting benefits. They began a fifty year experiment and called it the CORO FOUNDATION. This book is the story of how that enterprise unfolded.

WHY SHOULD YOU READ THIS BOOK?

The simple fact is, we still do not know how to govern ourselves. We do not understand what the relationship should be between citizens and their government. We do not know how to initiate youth into the body politic, and we do not know how to live peacefully with each other.

It's not for lack of interest, not for lack of trying. Tocqueville was right about that.

In their particular trying, W. Donald Fletcher and Van Duyn Dodge take us a good distance toward understanding how to set up educational experiences for citizens that, predictably, produce enthusiasm and dedication to public service. As you shall see in these pages, graduates of their program do, in fact, dedicate themselves to improving the quality of life in their communities; they do this consistently and over lifetimes.

Who should read this book? Coro graduates. The book is written from the special perspective of people who have had the "Coro experience"—Coro graduates. This experience is quite different from academic training which tends to focus on history, laws and institutional structures. Coro graduates have not just read about governance or studied processes; they have had first hand encounters that changed them and gave new directions to their lives. Reading this book should clarify Coro training for graduates so they can integrate it with their present experience and deepen their understanding of how they can continue to use Coro concepts and tools. Graduates will be tickled and amused and probably nostalgic to read about their colleagues.

Secondly, this story should be of keen interest to educators. Civic education in our country can only be characterized, for the most part, as "sterile". The excitement of campaigning, the intensity with which citizens pursue their special interests, the dedication which moves citizens to volunteer and to start up new non-profit services rarely seeps into state mandated civics classes. Something has gone amiss here. Coro methodology lends itself readily and economically to public school classrooms. Teachers can glimpse how to change the atmosphere of their classes through reading this book.

Thirdly, a great movement is afoot in this nation to renew civic life. The National Civic League, the National Association for Community Leadership, The Firethorn Institution and great Foundations such as The Kettering, Rockefeller, Ford and Danforth are all agents of this positive change. The keen interest these powerful organizations are bringing to this quest is evidence that many thoughtful people recognize that in this new age of mass equality and mass access to information systems, the work to be done to adapt our system of governance to these changed conditions lies before us. These organizations are searching for efforts that are not only well grounded conceptually but ones which also have proven records of success over years of time. Coro certainly qualifies, and this book introduces such seekers to the ideas and the record.

As you will find in the coming chapters, Coro Foundation began its first Internship in Public Affairs in 1947 in the City of San Francisco with eleven returning veterans who were financed by the G.I. Bill. Internships were unusual at the time and fell under the federal

Regard governing, they thought we could and must do better.

government's definition of vocational training. But, from the beginning, Coro was much more than on-the-job training; Coro offered a whole new way of looking at the public sector and of redefining the relationship between the citizen and government.

Coro was so successful in attracting young people to public service that the program expanded to Los Angeles in 1957, encouraged by a grant from Ford Foundation. In 1973, The Danforth Foundation made it possible for Coro to open a program in St. Louis, and in 1980, a New York Center was started up. The original ten month, full time Fellows program, was supplemented by many shorter term special programs, meeting the training needs of teachers, minorities, women, senior citizens, police, legislators and others.

By 1993, there were over 3,500 graduates of Coro programs, and over 75% of these graduates either worked in the public sector or served in appointive or elective positions. Coro graduates have served in every administration since Dwight Eisenhower's. Coro graduates sit in the House of Representatives, the U.S. Senate and are prominent in state and local government. Coro graduates are founders and directors of major national and community public interest organizations and they analyze complex public issues for respected publications across the country.

In addition to direct program participants, Coro programs each year involve hundreds of community leaders in their programs as field faculty, project mentors, mystery guests, selection judges, sponsors of community celebrations, donors and members of various boards and advisory councils. Taken altogether over the years, Coro's programs have involved tens of thousands of people in looking at governance issues and the quality of our democratic systems. This contribution is truly inestimable.

This book tells Coro's story to you in a Coroesque fashion, that is, not going directly from point "A" to point "B", for if we did that, we might never arrive where we wish to go. So we shall be round-a-bout. A favorite Coro metaphor is the story of the blind men and the elephant. Each person, feeling a different part of the animal, was convinced the whole animal was something quite different from the reality. But, in the quest for understanding, each seeker was alert and brought to the task the full range of his/her experience and insight. So we ask the reader to bring this kind of patience and this kind of focus to reading about Coro. The whole, after all, is there somewhere in the part.

The first section helps you get acquainted with Coro founders Mr. W. Donald Fletcher and Mr. Van Duyn Dodge. Mr. Fletcher speaks for himself, as has always been his privilege. We shall also introduce you to these gentlemen through the voices of others.

Section II includes graduates sharing anecdotes with you about their training experiences and telling some tall tales about the early days. Section III drops into some of the critical concepts and philosophy underlying Coro training and shares some methodology. Section VI chronicles the history of Coro and the more specific stories of each center. Section V allows you to meet quite a few Coro graduates, and recognize some public figures. Section VI shares the founder's and graduates' visions of the future, where they, Coro, and possibly this nation will be living just the day beyond next.

TRAINING FOR THE WIGGLY WORLD OF POLITICS

We live in a wiggly world.

In this world we never know what is going to happen next. We live with uncertainty, unpredictability, constant change. Everything is in motion around us—like the tide, the ripples on the water, the wind fluttering the leaves on the trees.

People come and go in our lives, creating, building, fragmenting, breaking and re-creating relationships. Events fall like rain into the evening news and morning paper. Even big, solid appearing institutions like government reveal their inner fluidity and shimmer before our eyes.

Just when we focus on one view and think we see it clearly, the vision dissolves like a cinematic image and re-emerges as a new picture.

No part of the world has more wiggles and squiggles than the part we label political.

The political part is somewhere near the center, and it is in this area that many of the wiggles begin to cross and converge.

People who want something, people who have ideas of what ought to be done work their way toward the center where they know they will find power and resources. Near the center they jostle and jiggle; they find allies or enemies; they put things together or they cast vetoes.

The wiggly world does not seem to be an accident that can be prevented nor something broken that can be repaired. The wiggly world is just being its natural self. We human beings are part of this world, and although we like to imagine we have things under control, and we go around making solemn pronouncements about new plans, as a matter of actual fact, we are as wiggly as anything else around.

So maybe we should stop trying to squeeze, constrict and stomp on all the spurty little squiggles and see if we can learn to go with the flow, dance to the rhythms, and wiggle at the best of all possible times.

What kind of citizen can live in such a world?

What kind of training can prepare a citizen to live in such a world?

W. Donald Fletcher

Van Duyn Dodge

4

The Founders

Education is the acquisition of the art of the utilization of knowledge.

Alfred North Whitehead

W. Donald Fletcher and Van Duyn A. Dodge founded Coro. They were a team. There is no doubt but that Coro would not have emerged without the two of them working and inspiring each other. Each of them has left a legacy that will always be a part of Coro. This section, devotes more space to Fletcher because Dodge left the scene in 1975, whereas Fletcher continues on twenty years later to this time of writing in 1995, still dreaming big dreams and working each day.

In this section, you will read a rare interview which Fletcher gave us, reflecting his special quality and style of thinking without the intervention of an editor. You will also read about Fletcher through the eyes of Coro staffers and Fellows. Finally you can meet Dodge, mostly as interpreted by Fletcher and Coro staffers.

Don Fletcher would never describe himself as a leader, and yet many men and women have changed the set of their lives because of their contact with him. Neither of the two organizations he founded, Coro or Liaison Citizens would have endured or retained their consistent purpose if it had not been for his influence, his modeling, his selfless service. Most of those who know Don and who have worked for him think of him as a leader.

He might consent to being called a teacher. Yet he is not the usual sort of teacher one thinks of. Consider comments by David Abel, Fellow and staffer:

I've had many educational experiences, including law school, and many teachers, but no teacher ever had the impact on me that WDF did. He made me do the thinking. I wasn't just trying to guess what he wanted me to say. After an encounter with Don, I'd think about it all the way home, trying to untangle what had happened. I was so motivated, I worked on reaching for understanding all the time. I was intrigued by the notion there might be a new way to think about politics. I haven't encountered that even though I have traveled in politics, academia, and in all the places where people are supposed to know about these things. Mostly the thinking seems to me to be repetitious, sterile, boring—the same patterns endlessly repeated. But Don still hasn't given up. He's on to something. I've never ceased trying to figure out what.

Alfred North Whitehead once said, "No language can be anything but elliptical, requiring a leap of imagination to understand its meaning in its relevance to immediate experience." But just hearing words does not bring meaning; one has to grow in experience until the words spring to life. An intuitive leap is required. The great teacher entices the learner to supply that imaginative leap. Suddenly the familiar becomes new; there is enlightenment. Ideas rearrange into new patterns. Change, growth, becomes possible.

Again quoting Whitehead: "The teacher has a double function. It is for him to elicit the enthusiasm by resonance from his own personality, and to create the environment of a larger knowledge and a firmer purpose."

Fletcher became an expert in such arousal. By staging a variety of new experiences for the learner, then asking questions no one had ever asked before, the experiences were thrown into new relationships. The learner had no book knowledge to rely upon, no teacher guide, nothing but his own real life experience and his native intelligence to lean upon. Tentatively, anxiously, the seeker began to seek for authentic responses from within his own field of intelligence — in short, he began to think. A student can never forget such a teacher. The experience is akin to being asleep for many years; then suddenly awakening to a different world, no longer dim, but sparkling and abrim with possibilities.

Another skill Fletcher mastered was listening. When he leaned forward and fixed you with his intent gaze and smiled his expectant smile, you felt that the next words you uttered just might be pregnant with meaning, even though, at the moment, you did not know what they might be.

Through this process, repeated many times, of being surprised, put on center stage, questioned, built up, let down, all in the quizzical company of your fellows, amazingly, you gained confidence and began to think in an independent way.

You never felt in an encounter with Don that he was behaving this way in a deliberate effort to change you. That would have raised resistance. No, you felt he did it all out of an intense interest in something, part of which was your reactions. You felt somehow you were on an important mutual quest for some insight so significant, the world might be changed.

Some students who had mastered the skill of giving back to teachers what they wanted to hear and who had always been rewarded with praise and top grades were frustrated and baffled by the Fletcherian approach. Some never forgave him. But others, like David Abel and many whom you will meet in this book, give Don their highest praise: *He woke me up. He made me think.*

BACK AND FORTH, AN INTERVIEW WITH W. DONALD FLETCHER

Coro, what it was and what it became, is intertwined with the thinking and character of its founders. Fran Aleshire, Allan Gershman, and Ben Neufeld interviewed Don Fletcher in January of 1991, curious as to what led to his long quest and wanting to know more about him and Dodge as men. Additional material came from an interview Jim Schoning conducted with Fletcher in 1982.

Growing Up Years

Question: Judging from many of the questions you ask, you seem to have a rural background.

Don: Yes, I worked as a farmhand for my uncle many summers in Eastern Oregon. I plowed fields behind six horses, cut and bound hay, gathered it up and then went back and uprooted the weeds. I learned to respect what it took to manage a successful farm.

Question: Where did you live the rest of the year?

Don: I lived on a residential street in Portland, with only two or three houses to the block. My sister was three years younger than I, and thirteen years later, I got a younger brother. I lived very happily with my parents. Grammar school was just six blocks away and later I bicycled to high school.

Question: What did you do for fun in those days?

Don: Life was good. I was never sick, and I took part in all kinds of sports: baseball, soccer, handball, especially handball. Oregon was a wild country at that time, so I spent many days hiking the Cascades and swimming the Columbia. The Columbia was a mile wide in front of our place. We used to start upstream and see if we could swim to shore before the current carried us too far. One time I was astonished to stand up in the middle of the river, and find I was only knee deep. To this day, I try to swim every week.

Question: Did anything unusual happen?

Don: Yes, my mother died in 1928 when I was twenty, some sort of kidney trouble. The next year my father suddenly died of spinal meningitis. He was just 51. In those days medical knowledge was not so good, and I don't think we would have lost either of them today. It was quite a shock. A wonderful maiden aunt came to live with us. My sister and I were old enough to go off to college, but my younger brother was adopted by my uncle, a professor at Colorado University.

Question: Tell us a little more about your family background.

Don: My great grandfather on my mother's side came to Portland because the Columbia River reminded him of the Rhine where he had grown up. He homesteaded land and found it ideal for farming. He had four sons and three daughters to take care of the farm, so he spent more of his time reading. My grandfather on my father's side had a small farm. Just about everyone farmed for a living in those days.

Question: And your father and mother?

Don: They were both able to go to college. In fact they met at the University of the Pacific. My father got a master's degree from Columbia and became principal of a school in Pueblo, Colorado. I was born there in 1908. My parents didn't like the Colorado climate, so they returned to Portland in 1910.

Question: Tell us a little more about your parents. Were they politically minded, religious, what?

Don: My father was a very good school principal. I became aware of "politics" one evening when my father got a phone call, and I saw red going up his neck. It seems a political machine in Portland was trying to persuade him to run for Superintendent of Schools, but he wouldn't do it. We had some pretty good discussions, but I didn't think much about politics. I was more an athlete. My father was a religious person, a member of the Unitarian Church. But he let his children decide for themselves, and I just went to church once in awhile. My mother was a superb homemaker and stayed at home as most women did.

College Days

Question: So when your parents died, you were on your own just ready to go to college. Where did you go?

Don: I went to Reed College, a small liberal arts school, of about 400 students, known today as somewhat radical. The faculty was very fine. I lived with a relative, and a friend picked me up in a Model T and drove us to school. Remember we were in the midst of a Depression, and everyone scrimped.

W. Donald Fletcher

My father was a very good school principal. I became aware of "politics" one evening when my father got a phone call, and I saw red going up his neck. It seems a political machine in Portland was trying to persuade him to run for Superintendent of Schools, but he wouldn't do it.

Question: You went two years to Reed and then what?

Don: I wanted to go to Stanford, but I had to earn money to go there. I looked around for work in the Spring of 1927 and ended up keeping books in the afternoons for an ice cream company and making deliveries at night. I saved almost every dime I made.

Question: Then you went to Stanford?

Don: Yes, as a junior transfer. It was most enjoyable, more social than Reed, a real treat. I lived in a little house near campus and then joined a fraternity. I majored in the social sciences which meant you could take just about anything. I found Stanford had a humor magazine, the *Chaparral,* and they needed a business manager. The position was paid and came with board and room besides. That intrigued me. I made a nice hunk of money, and I got acquainted with business people in San Francisco.

Travels Abroad

Question: What happened after you graduated?

Don: Well, I'd gotten acquainted with a Terry LaCroix, a big, burly guy who worked for the Dollar Line. Along about August, he said, "Well, Don, could you be ready in about ten days to go to sea?' I said, "I sure could." So I got on board the President Garfield, ahead of the privileged son sponsored by a California senator. I appreciated that. I saw the world isn't all run by favoritism, so I went around the world by sea.

Question: What was the trip like?

Don: For one thing, the Dollar Line stocked up on food six months ahead of time, so I lost a lot of weight. We sailed to Hawaii and then hit a pretty good typhoon off Japan. Very enjoyable. I remember the rain in Japan and the wooden shoes people wore to stay above the water in the streets. We continued on around to world to Manila, Egypt, Genoa, Marseilles, New York, Panama and Los Angeles.

Question: Was that the end of your overseas experience?

Don: No, I got the idea of going to the London School of Economics, and I pestered people until I turned up a free ride to London. I audited classes for awhile, then went to the continent and bicycled through Europe.

Question: Wait a minute. What attracted you to the London School of Economics?

Don: I really can't say where ideas come from, they just float around up here. I wasn't in pursuit of any idea or anything in particular, I just wanted to see Europe.

Question: Did anything about the London school impress you?

Don: Not much. I remember one professor who intrigued me. He said, "No matter how hard you try or how good your luck is, you'll never accomplish anything." He was a gloomy kind. He was very serious. He was saying, "You people don't count for much. " We talked quite a bit about what he really meant.

Question: What did you think?

Don: I can't remember, but he made us think. What did he mean by his crazy statements? Young men are supposed to accomplish things.

Question: So then you bicycled through Europe?

Don: That's right. I bought a bicycle for $9.73 and sold it for $8.50 and went 3,400 miles. I left England with $600. I bought a fine suit, which I still have and value highly, and got back to New York with $450.

Question: Where did you stay at night?

Don: Remember, it was the bottom of the Depression, but they had youth hostels. You could stay in a castle for 10 cents a night. They'd give you a pallet and a blanket and low cost food, and that was it.

Question: You did all this entirely on your own?

Don: Yes, but I want to say one thing. Robert E. Swing was Acting President of Stanford, and I heard he'd been educated in Germany, so I went to see him before I left. He was a wonderful person and gave me all kinds of information.

Question: You went to see the President of the university for an itinerary?

Don: Yes, why not?

Question: Seems a little unusual.

Don: Must have been due to my personality. No, I have found presidents are very fine individuals who are happy to help students.

Question: But most students don't know that. Well, getting on, after taking this year out, you returned to the U.S. and entered Stanford Law School?

Don: That's right.

Question: What kind of education did you get there?

Don: We had high quality professors who challenged me to think. The attrition rate was high. I was a little older than the other students, so I was offered a free room if I would be a "mature" presence for the boys. But I enjoyed the social and athletic activities so much that the Dean called me in for a little visit in December. The Dean said, "Don, I'm not sure you know what you are here for." I agreed with him since my grades hovered around D.

I moved out of the fraternity and rented an apartment with several friends. By April, I was in the top 20% and stayed there. This made an impression on me, but I realized there was still a big difference between the top 10% and 20%. The top students seem to grasp things much quicker.

Question: Didn't they just study harder?

Don: No, they caught on more easily. One of my bright colleagues became Dean of the Law School. Some had been raised with great advantages, parents who were attorneys, and so on.

Question: Did you specialize?

Don: No, just general law.

Question: Any interest in politics?

Don: Not really. Of course Fascism was becoming a threat in Europe, and we weren't unaware, but college students were not wrapped up in the day's events.

Entry Into the Work World

Question: Did you practice law when you graduated?

Don: I got an offer from Fitzgerald, Adam and Beardsley, all from Stanford, and I worked for them while I studied for the Bar Exam. After passing, I worked for a small two-man law firm, A. B. Bianchi. Bianchi was a fine gentleman who loved taking offbeat cases. Only one third of our class got jobs, so I was lucky, and I enjoyed working there for two years. Then I got a higher paid job at $75/month with an insurance company.

Question: During this time were you able to think about getting married and starting a family?

Don: You are back to assuming planning on my part. Actually it is quite a story. There aren't many paying jobs during a depression, but you can always get a job selling things. So I picked up a job selling silk hosiery in 1933. I went door to door in Atherton, an area with lots of rich people. I drove into this fancy driveway and met

I remember one professor who intrigued me . . . He made us think. What did he mean by his crazy statements?

the lady of the house who invited me in. She was very nice, a quality person. Pretty soon she said, "I want you to meet my daughter, Louise," so I met my future wife, Louise, selling silk stockings. Very romantic.

Question: What happened next?

Don: I had a rule not to go out with females more than once every three weeks because I was too busy selling, but I made an exception and delivered the order when it came through. I saw Louise again and of course one thing led to another, and we were married in 1936.

Question; How did you get involved in the Willkie campaign?

Don: Well I had intended setting up my own law firm, but the campaign interested me, and I got sidetracked.

Question: What about Willkie attracted you so strongly?

Don: Remember again, this was not planned, I'm not that way. I just didn't like what Franklin Roosevelt was doing in packing the Supreme Court. Then some good friends of mine were working on the campaign, and they were having trouble getting volunteers in San Jose. I thought I could help them, I had friends there. Also Willkie just intrigued me, caught my attention.

Question: How much time did you spend on the campaign?

Don: About six months. After that, I had to find something else. I got to know Van Duyn Dodge quite well about this time, and I was very interested in his way of thinking and speaking. Dodge could size people up quickly and easily. I remember one luncheon where one fellow was a real stuffed shirt. Van Duyn spent thirty minutes talking about the various uses of salt, and the fellow never realized he was being had. Dodge was so interesting, no one could take offense.

Question: What do you think Dodge saw in you?

Don: Well, I think it was my knack of jumping way out here and way out there, this idea thing I've been talking about. I'd come up with something, and Van Duyn would check it out.

Question: You weren't frustrated because one was thinking so differently from the other?

Don: No, I enjoyed him, and he enjoyed me. I'm not analytical. That goes to the nine-tenths. Have I explained that?

Question: No, shoot.

Don: Basic proposition. Particularly in the political world, of our total intelligence, nine-tenths is unconscious. We judge people at a submerged level. I have learned in dealing with uneducated kids, you have to deal at this level. Dodge and I related very well on this level.

Question: How did you encounter John Dewey?

Don: Reading was a habit with me. I was interested in education, and Dewey made sense, especially how you deal with uneducated people. Van Duyn and I felt we were in a ferment of ideas, and we exchanged books and ideas frequently.

The Research Period and Founding Coro

Question: So then it was after the Willkie campaign that you and Dodge decided to research the area of citizenship and governance?

Don: Talking to businessmen during the campaign, I was impressed with how angry they were about government. I thought they needed a better connection with City Hall. My original idea was something like Ralph Nader's, create a pressure group and tell public officials what to do. But I attended a post-election rally of Willkie supporters, and I was very disappointed in their plans. So I began talking more seriously with Van Duyn.

Question: We are now into 1941. What was Dodge's approach?

Don: He said, "Don, why don't we look into the system and find out how it works?"

Question: How were you able to proceed?

Don: The Mills family had a building, and they gave us offices on the 14th floor for free. So we could begin some serious research.

Question: What was the role of General Semantics at this time?

Don: Van Duyn had read Korzybski's *Science and Sanity* and thought it very sound. These ideas helped provide an approach to our field work but mostly we just did what Coro does, we went out and wandered around. We were intrigued by the labor people because of their constant struggle to get what they wanted. They were politically astute and more interesting to talk to than the businessmen who were politically unaware. I always found it easy and enjoyable to talk to public officials.

Then Dodge and I would discuss what we were learning.

Question: What did you learn in questioning people?

Don: I found each group had a structure for their thinking. If you talked to a business person in New York or in Los Angeles, you'd get about the same responses. Same with labor and government. After a time, you are not learning anything new. You can almost predict what people will say.

Question: Did you study public meetings?

Don: Yes, we attended many meetings of the San Francisco Board of Supervisors, and again, we could begin to see patterns, predictable behavior. About this time, we got a boost when Garfield Shafer joined us. He had studied under Freud in Vienna and he brought in the issue of the unconscious. He volunteered to study the Board meetings, and after awhile, he could predict how decisions were going to go. There seemed to be structures, which the participants were unaware of, which mastered their behavior.

Question: Tell us a little more about what you were learning from your research and how you went about it.

Don: If you start assuming you know nothing, that is a good place to begin. You're not that easily misled, and you begin to see relationships between language and culture. That is what Korzybski explains. I must have read him five or six times. There's our basic map. We were interested in the sanity of our society. Political behavior is one of the facets, that's all. We had no political science orientation. We didn't want to be bothered by all that stuff. We wanted to figure things out from observation, so we spent three years just educating ourselves.

Question: Did you and Dodge agree on a course of action?

Don: We early decided that an organization was needed to research the role of citizens, but unfortunately we couldn't get funding and we were at a point where we had to bring in money. Dean Edwin Coltrell from Stanford, who was on our Board, suggested we think about an internship program for returning veterans and get funding from the G. I. Bill. Jean Witter, from the brokerage firm, made the same suggestion. So Van

We wanted to figure out from observation, so we spent three years educating ourselves.

Congressman Jack Shelley and
W. Donald Fletcher

Duyn and I checked out all the internship programs and found they were all very academic. I didn't think they were accomplishing much.

Question: So you were able to overcome organizational and funding problems and begin the first Internship in Public Affairs in the year of 1947–48?

Don: That's right. We began the Internship with myself as trainer/director and three additional trainers. Some of the local universities cooperated, and we began the laboratory courses. The City and County of San Francisco authorized their people to accept Interns, and we were a going concern.

Question: Other than the G.I. Bill, what other support did you get in those early days?

Don: That's important. Van Duyn put in $250,000 over the years, and I worked without pay and put in money besides. We had some excellent friends on our Board of Trustees, and many friends who kept our spirits up. I'd go into see my friends at Standard Oil, Pacific Gas and Electric, Bank of America, and they'd encourage me.

This goes to the roots of Coro.

Question: Why did they help?

Don: I didn't ask. They just saw a young attorney and a respected financial manager trying to do something, and that sums it up. They liked what we said. They'd been around enough to know what needed to be done. Later, we had a much harder time in Los Angeles because we didn't know anyone.

Question: What was it like to work with the returning veterans in the early internships?

Don: Challenging these young people was a lot of fun for me. I had more experience behind me intellectually than they did, perhaps. Some of them had very determined views, and it was fun to push and pull on those views. This probably helped shape subsequent internships.

Question: Did you have a guiding philosophy?

Don: No, I believe that a guiding philosophy has to develop from within each person. You develop it out of experience. Let me explain. I learned patience from Dodge. He had a way of listening and analyzing what others said, a persistence in looking at many sides of a question, and he knew the importance of evaluating the kind of language being used. As I went into the interviewing process, listening to dozens of people from all sectors of the community, I became aware of the "native soil" of community life and of how the democratic process worked.

Question: How did you teach the Interns to approach the field, the community?

Don. I wanted our trainees to learn how to discover for themselves, not to follow some formula. This fits in with the basic tenet of freedom to think, which requires an ability to discover for oneself. Within the first hour of the Internship, the trainee was involved in various physical challenges which required him to look, listen, sense and guess what was going on.

Question: And how does this relate to public affairs?

Don: The Internship was a microcosm of society and public affairs. We involved the trainees in a series of group challenges where the responsibility of each person was both individual and collective. These strangers experienced each other's attitudes toward many factors — economic, social and political. All at once they were in the midst of discussion, decision-making, reporting, etc. We didn't tell them that. We simply threw them in the water and told them to swim the best they could.

Question: What happened?

Don: The Interns found themselves fascinated by all kinds of information in the field, without the benefit of an academic structure. Each began to slowly and surely develop a sense of values and expectations related to what society requires in the conduct of public affairs. They were creating their own philosophical base, largely pragmatic and not concerned with orthodox dogma.

Question: Did they develop a Coro philosophy?

Don: No. The Coro staff tried to avoid that. Instead, we used every means to enrich or to stimulate new ways of observing, listening and sensing what influenced public affairs. Thus drama, literature, field trips, constant discussions, all became the bill of fare to which Interns became accustomed.

Question: Sounds like you are stating your own educational philosophy.

Don: Exactly. Coro is an educational institution. Our role is to prepare capable young people wherein they will be creating/participating in public affairs dynamics — as they interpret the needs and means present.

A Founder's View of the Future

Question: What does Coro need to do to prepare for the future?

Don: I'd like to see some of our seasoned graduates undertake the kind of research Dodge and I did fifty years ago. People in public affairs today need a new vision of what life is all about. Too many of our public officials lack originality; they lack vision; they lack an intellectual base. Coro could do a good deal about this.

Question: I've heard you say Coro needs to upgrade what is going on.

Don: "Upgrade" may not be the best word. We need more light. We know the struggle that goes on to interpret scientific data. There are tremendous energies set loose in the political area but little understanding of how to deal with these energies.

Question: What makes this necessary?

Don: All the messes in the world. It's clear. We need a different intellectual base. There isn't enough money to deal with it in the usual political way. We waste millions of dollars erasing graffiti. That's stupid. We don't know how to govern ourselves, that's what it adds up to. We won't get change without the necessary thinking. Coro people are prepared to do that. I'd like to see this project go forward. Let the research team create their own project. Start no place and go some-place. They know the Coro dynamics. It's up to them to create interpretations. When they are done, let the rest of us comment. Why not?

SOMETHING ABOUT VAN DUYN DODGE

Fifty years from the beginning of Coro, we can only know Van Duyn A. Dodge through the eyes of those who knew him. We suspect that Coro would not have happened without this dedicated individual. The following comments will give the reader some insights about him.

W. D. Fletcher describes Van Duyn as "a practical philosopher, an individual seeking methods to improve things, not just talking about what happens and how it happens, but what can you do about it." Dodge was deeply impressed with *Science and Sanity* by Alfred

Van Duyn A. Dodge at early GS Seminar

Korzybski. In it he found a whole new idea of how man deals with his destiny and how people behave. He was much interested in the "sanity factor" of the public and how we can bring more intelligence, more awareness, into the process of public affairs.

Dodge had been an accountant and from that discipline learned a very tight form of analysis. He wanted to see how things fit together. He had developed an excellent reputation in the small town of Modesto working for Standard Oil. He quickly rose to become head of the Accounting Department but then went to San Francisco to found his own brokerage firm. He became a pioneer in investment management. Frank Aleshire and other Interns recall the advice Van Duyn gave them — to start putting money aside monthly in a mutual fund, so they would become wealthy later. The Dodge/Cox Fund was an early entry into the mutual fund industry, and it has compiled a fine success history.

A Gentleman of the Old School

Fletcher explains that Dodge came from an educated family. His father, Nathan Dodge, was a gentleman of the old school, clear minded, knowledgeable about economics and keenly interested in world affairs. Dodge grew up in an atmosphere where he was well trained in how to examine things. Fletcher was fascinated by Dodge's method of questioning and reasoning, and he credits his friend with causing a major shift in his thinking. The two were well suited to reason together; Fletcher supplied the dynamic uplift, and Dodge connected them to the earth. Fletcher comments, "Dodge had a facility for asking simple questions and then going into the ramifications of what those simple questions led into. He could never be crowded or bulldozed in his thinking. You could advance what you thought was a brilliant idea, and he'd look at it very carefully, and at the end of a few days that idea would be thoroughly explored if it had any merit."

Dodge had unusual work habits, according to Fletcher. He got to work at 10AM, took a long lunch and went home at 8PM. After a short period of reading and a nap, he worked until 4AM. He enjoyed this pattern because it gave him solitude and time to think.

Commenting on Coro, Dodge said: " Coro Foundation is not political. It is not partisan. It is not taking sides on any social or economic question or proposal. It is not being for or against certain pressure groups. It is straightforward, constructive work. It is of such a nature that others can make no political capital out of opposing the work. It is done in the name of the public welfare. It is done in the name of social morale. It can be done continuously — not limited to election periods."

Fletcher summed up his feeling for his friend: "It seems to me that our country has countless individuals who play key roles in keeping our country on a sound track. This type tends to shun publicity, feeling fully compensated simply from performing worthwhile service to society. They invest themselves, their dreams, and their abilities. Such a person was Van Duyn A. Dodge."

Dodge was born in 1897 and died in 1975 at the age of 78. He was a native San Franciscan, co-founder of Dodge & Cox, and a co-founder of Coro in 1942. His will requested memorial contributions go to Coro. He was the steady hand and guide of Coro, a good friend to many Coro Interns, and an outstanding citizen.

Mental cultivation is nothing less than the satisfactory way in which the mind will function when it is poked into activity.

Alfred North Whitehead

Van Duyn A. Dodge

FLETCHER AND DODGE FROM DIFFERENT PERSPECTIVES

It is proverbial that institutions are lengthened shadows of the founding genius or geniuses. You might agree if you knew W. Donald Fletcher and Van Duyn Dodge and then checked into the training methods still in use by Coro. The methods continue to be unique and often baffling to participants. Here are comments from those who knew these men the best and who saw them in action.

The Coro Way

by Bill Whiteside, SF '54

Executive Director, LA

Being opinionated, it was hard for me to learn the Coro staff role, of creating learning opportunities rather than expounding. This method was firmly rooted in the educational principle that 'discovery' gives ownership to a lesson and in the General Semantics concept that the 'map' (descriptive words) is not the 'territory' (the phenomena). Navigating in the complex territory of public life, you needed first hand acquaintance with the territory.

Don made me memorize Alexander Pope's "Dictum:"

Men should be taught as though one taught them not, things unknown proposed as things forgot.

I remember a notable summer when Don led the staff through a week-long seminar on Korzybski's *Science and Sanity.* Don had a way of inspiring individual performance. One exercise, for example, was to direct our attention away from areas in our own background and force us to consider subject matter world's away from what we knew. The assignments ranged from Zen to Alice in Wonderland to classical music. Our minds were profoundly "opened" to new points of view and ways of thinking.

Although Don Fletcher had a greater impact on me than anyone except my father, I don't want to leave the impression all was easy. During my fifteen years on the Coro staff, there were scores of occasions when the staff thoughtfully planned a Friday seminar, an orientation or a selection, and Don would arrive with a NEW PLAN, one that he had developed between 3:00 and 7:00AM, complete with scripts for staff. It didn't make it any easier to admit that his new version was more successful than the outcome of our rehashed exercise might have been.

The Twinkle in His Eyes

by Sam Sewall, 1924–1992, SF '49, Trainer

I believe it was the twinkle in his eyes.

Certainly it wasn't the salary: little as it was, Coro staffers in 1948 quickly learned that their salaries wouldn't always get paid on time and would never compete with "regular" jobs moneywise.

And it wasn't the glory: Coro was clearly regarded by "practical" people, my family included, as some sort of pipe dream that had very little hope of realizing even its own survival much less its idea of influencing the effectiveness of government.

No, the reason that we gave up being administrative assistants in government (jobs we had thought we'd sell our souls to acquire) in order to help Don Fletcher hold this fledgling effort together was the twinkle in his eyes.

It was there when he told us the difference we could make. And, when after outlining some magnificent goal, he'd say, "Now, you can make that happen, can't you, Sam?" I thought I just might. Heady stuff for a 23-year-old!

I think the twinkle in his eye came from the fun he had watching people react to having familiar concepts turned inside out, upside down; stuffy pedantries proven false-to-fact or non-survival oriented. He liked seeing people raise their vision of what they expected of themselves or others.

Come to think of it, how many people do you know who kept their twinkle all their life long? Personally, life has never since held for me that special excitement that was part of working with Don Fletcher—yes, and promise, too!

He Knows the Secret, or Does He?

by Austin Woodward, SF '52, Staff, LA

I'll always think of him as "WDF" because that was the signature he used on his inter-staff memos, which called us to attention and alerted us to a session coming up and what our role was to be. My being "in the docket" raised my blood pressure, and if my session was right before or after WDF's, it was like trying to give a speech following Martin Luther King or playing the trumpet on the same platform as Louis Armstrong.

How did WDF capture our attention? It wasn't just a happy accident. I've seen him do it with all sorts of people and in all sorts of settings. I suppose there were some tricks. My wife, Rosalie, recalls how he opened one session with her: "Now, Rosalie, where's the beginning?" Other classics were: "Mr. Woodward, how do you decide which club to use when playing a 175-par 3 in a crosswind at Pebble Beach?" or, "Mr. Jones, what's the ideal number of instruments in a Dixieland band, and does it matter if you are two short?" We all dreaded these questions, and our anxiety kept us on our toes mentally. We had to pay attention or be hung out to dry when the spotlight focused on us.

Later, I realized there were no right answers, but during all the time I worked with him, I felt strongly that WDF was in possession of a rare secret—which some day would be mine.

Give Them a Poke
an interview with John Greenwood, LA '68
Executive Director, LA

John: I think one of the pure joys of working with Don Fletcher as a trainer is never knowing what is going to happen next, whether the "trick" is going to work. And I don't think Don really knows if it is going to work either.

Question: Perhaps that is the point. Everything he does grows out of a genuine curiosity in his own mind as to what might happen. As he says: "If nothing interesting is happening, give them a poke." When you begin a discussion with a group, you notice people right away fall into a stereotypical mode of reasoning. Don has discovered that you have to give people a poke to jar them out of this bad habit. He prods here and pokes there until he gets some action going, and then the fun begins.

John: Agreed, I'm sure if he knew in advance how the conversation was going to go, he'd lose all interest. When I was preparing to become a trainer for a new leadership program in L.A., I consulted with Don. He said, "You know, John, you're going to have to do some deep thinking." He was right. Thinking in the Fletcherian sense means coming up with something just a half inch out of the culture. It has to be invented new. There's no easy, no lazy way to do this.

Question: You're talking about a different role for the trainer, contrary to theory. It is frightening to encounter a new mix of people without a lesson plan. But in Don's view, if you use the same old lesson plans and end up in the same old place, no one learns anything.

John: That's right, it's scary but intensely interesting, too. Don lets you know he's having fun with you, and when the atmosphere begins to tense up, he finds a way to let the stale air out. When the discussion turns ponderous, you can detect the thought going through Don's mind: "This isn't fun anymore, we have to do something." Coro or LC sessions have this quality of play, of discovery, of surprise.

Question: Can one learn how to use this technique?
John: To a degree, yes, but it all must come from an intense curiosity that is utterly sincere, a self-confidence that enjoys taking risks and a zest for games, drama and competition. The game's the thing!

Don's Dialogue
by Fran Aleshire

Life experiences that are truly memorable and transforming have to have some quality about them that is deeply personal. You have to discover hidden powers in yourself or suddenly see something with new eyes. I think getting caught up in one of Don Fletcher's games can be powerful for these reasons.

The beginning moves in the play are pretty ordinary. You say the expected things, and others reply in formal, stereotypical patterns. Ho, hum. But then the pace picks up. The odd questions unfold: "What does the newborn know about economics?" "Is it better to plow with the curve of the hill or away from it?" "Do you really think or just think that you think?" Ordinary responses aren't really possible to such questions, and you and the others sitting in the circle find yourselves reaching into new mental crevices and at times coming up with an extraordinary thought.

The ideas come out fresher, clearer and ever more interesting, and you focus intently, listen more raptly. Perhaps you and "they" are not what you thought, nor is "thinking" what you assumed it to be. Occasionally you, and perhaps the group, undergo that transforming moment of new insight, of change. You may not understand what has happened, but you know it had something to do with Don Fletcher and his method of training and this program called Coro, and you begin an inquiry that can last a whole life to find out what it is that turns an ordinary human being into someone truly extraordinary.

Van Duyn Dodge, The Steady Hand

by Jerry Jones, SF '52, Trainer,

Executive Director, SF

Van Duyn had a great gift of comprehension. He took in more than most people ever saw; he could discern the ripple effect of changes, so he could predict consequences. He seemed able to grasp all the elements which were germane to a situation, to have thoroughly examined every facet. He just turned every element of a situation over and over until he understood it.

Van Duyn was the one who introduced General Semantics to Don Fletcher. He sensed that an intellectual base was needed for the training program and a way to deal with the ambiguities that are so much a part of the political system. General Semantics provided him with the analytical structure he needed, and he thought man's entrapment in language accounted for much of the insanity he saw in politics. He wasn't a great cause person; he just wanted to bring more sanity to public affairs.

It was Dodge who was intrigued with the interaction of form and function in organizations and probably Dodge who conceived of such models as Load/Design/Working Parts/Fuel. Don Fletcher was always reaching far out for ideas, but Van Duyn was the one to take the ideas, work them over, and make them practical training tools.

I expect Don would have just wanted to turn the early Interns loose and let them discover whatever they might while Van Duyn would be challenged by devising ways to help the Interns talk about and analyze what they were experiencing.

They were a great team, just balancing each other. Aside from this, Dodge was the early major funder. He was an expert financier, a pioneer of mutual funds, and a founding partner in Dodge and Cox. I recall his fatherly advice to Interns to start investment programs. He was always the steady hand, the seasoned thinker. He died in November, 1975 and has been missed ever since.

I believe it was
the twinkle
in his eye . . .

Sam Sewall

Van Duyn Dodge and
W. Donald Fletcher

Something to Change Your Life

by Frank Aleshire, SF 47,
Trainer 1948–50

It's what we are all seeking, isn't it? Something to give depth and meaning to our lives? I'm reminded of yeast. Without certain experiences, life is flat. Nothing stands out, but sometimes things happen to you that change that. Coro was one of those experiences for me, so rich and poignant that seeds sprouted from it and grew in unexpected directions. Instead of just stumbling along, happening on a treasure here and there, I experienced the Coro people gathering together a whole cornucopia of impressions, ideas and activities which they dumped on me in a compressed period of time. The results were explosive and compelling. Later in life I realized something powerful had changed my life, but I wasn't sure what or how.

The Dynamics of a Community

by Uriel Manheim, SF 51

Coro entered my life when I saw a one page announcement posted on the bulletin board at the University of California, Berkeley. It wasn't much, but it changed my life.

Don Fletcher gave me two guidelines to use when analyzing the dynamics of a community. They made a big impression on me because Don emphasized them in many ways. One, he said to look for the power structure. "Who is in charge" will give you the clues you need to find your way and get things done. You can't always figure this out by just getting the names of the elected officials. You also have to know how to look in places you don't usually look. This leads to the second guideline.

The community is made up of different groups, which usually think quite differently one from the other. In the 40's, in San Francisco, labor was a big player, along with government and business. By placing us in these different groups, Coro interns learned the thinking patterns and values of each one. We could then move freely among them and sometimes act as interpreters.

These guidelines have helped me feel at home wherever I live and work.

GROWING UP WITH DON FLETCHER

Tomas McFletcher, Don Fletcher's son, now a management consultant in Scottsdale, Arizona, casts more insight on the relationship of a growing learner to Don, his father. Tomas served in the Peace Corps in Central America and was also a San Francisco Fellow. All of the Fletcher offspring are in education, one way or another.

Driven by Theory and Ideas

One of my most lasting impressions of ages 9 through 15 is of hearing the manual typewriter in the study when I woke up each Saturday and, commonly, Sunday morning. My room was next to the study, and there would be my dad, typing away on some theory or other. His usual greeting, if I was brave enough to stick my head into the study on those mornings was to ask some esoteric question such as, "Tom, what do you suppose the beggars in San Francisco are upset over?" Of course after a few of these, I would find a way to tiptoe away down the hall and into the kitchen for breakfast and then make my get away as quickly as I could because I knew. . . .

A Compulsion to Work

My sisters and I would soon be recruited to do "chores" around the place, which often meant pulling weeds in the spring, irrigating in the summer and raking in the fall. By the age of 11 I had complete responsibility for tending to 100 Leghorn hens. I was to raise the chickens, peddle the eggs to neighbors, keep records on expenses and sales and slaughter the birds for the family. As a typical teenager, I sometimes forgot to mind my responsibilities and would be reminded, usually on a weekend, when I would find myself cleaning out the henhouse.

At the same time, every weekend my dad would be working on some kind of project outside. These ranged from ploughing the 2.5 acres to sawing down trees to putting in new irrigation pipes or spraying fruit trees. He didn't like the routine things like sweeping the pool or mowing lawns, so this was hired out or passed on to the kids, but there was relief from time to time.

A Love of Travel

Weather permitting, we frequently went up into the hills behind Stanford University for afternoon picnics, or we might just go for a drive. Each summer we visited Oregon and Washington to visit relatives. A favorite spot was Neskowin on the Oregon Coast where we had the same cabin each summer. Dad played golf several times a day, and I caddied for him, but we still had time for picnics and walks on the beach.

Nothing was spared to teach a lesson.

Always Teaching, Always Learning, Always Pushing for Independence

Nothing was spared to teach a lesson. At age eleven, papa persuaded me to attend a Menlo Park City Council session because "I might learn something." I learned about bonds needed for sewers but not much about how to be a better baseball player which is where my mind was stuck at the time.

Traveling in the car, papa was a virtual encyclopedia on plants, terrain, climates, crops and animal life as we passed through one area of the country to another. I confess, to this day, I do the same thing.

Sometimes his lessons backfired, especially when he tried to use our mother as pupil. She had her own mind about things, but I noticed later that she pretty much went along if it made sense, after registering her objections.

Papa also stressed my independence. By 8 or 9 I was taking the train alone to San Francisco, and shortly thereafter, I went alone by train to Oregon.

Always the Frugal Scot

Often, my dad would point to his Scottish ancestry and his inherited frugality. Every Sunday night was shoe polish night, and we would see shoes of his that were 30 years old but still in good shape. His personal possessions were remarkably few and contained in just a few drawers, but what he had, he maintained, even after they fell from fashion. He just had a certain economy about him that we all have adopted.

The Fletcher Legacy

My dad has always been driven to sacrifice himself to lift up the community through political interaction. He always wanted to improve things. In so many ways he has made a difference in the lives of people through his community approach. Everytime he has seen people working and collaborating together, he is very pleased, very gratified. He has been trying to find a set of finger holes that could be set down and transmitted in such a way that people could find them and climb into the light. He has an almost naive belief that people have unlimited talent within that just needs to be liberated.

He's sacrificed every material comfort to this quest and never deviated from his high ideals. He looks for the good in people and is keenly appreciative when he sees growth and competence. His whole life has this consistent thrust.

Tall Tales and Yarns about Coro

If Coro training methodology could be explained by a bald statement of technique, a laying out of the facts, then all would have been explained long ago. But as is true of all great educational experiences — the basics are profoundly simple while the telling of "how to" is mystifyingly complex. "Experiential education" is just that; the experience itself brings about the shift in awareness, the awakening of understanding. Hence the experience cannot be imploded into words, but, rather, tends to explode into what? More experience!

For these reasons, the greatest of teachers have turned to parables, anecdotes, examples, stories, metaphors, leaving the reader to grasp the principles according to the level of his receptivity.

A Coro Fellow tries to relate to you something of the intriguing quality of his Internship. He struggles for words, says, "Well, you just have to have been there," and, finally, he tells you a story.

So here are a few good stories about Coro to help you know more about Coro than you know now.

TURNING THE TABLES ON WDF?
by John Greenwood, LA '68

Some times the Fellows couldn't resist trying to turn the tables on WDF, to see if they could make him squirm.

I remember one seminar in LA. We were in desperate financial straits and were occupying a rather seedy office at 5th and Spring Streets. There was a guy standing on the corner every day with a Bible in his hand. He screamed scripture at the top of his lungs. One time I went to him and said, "You know if you would just speak more softly, people would listen to you." All that got me was ten minutes of even more enraged screaming.

The Fellows thought it would be fun to invite this fellow up to the office for an interview. They gave him a slip of paper with directions and told him Don Fletcher wanted to find out how he could be saved. So this person, all disheveled and disturbed, came up to the office and asked for Don. I didn't know what was going on, but I could see the Fellows were grinning and twittering.

The receptionist called Don in, and after talking to the man for a few minutes, Don assembled the Fellows and said, "This gentleman has come to see me, and I'd like you all to interview him."

So we sat him down. He stopped screaming, and for thirty minutes he behaved in a completely normal and rational manner. Don Fletcher never let on that anything unusual was taking place. The Fellows were totally subdued, and I'm thinking, "Who is this Don Fletcher anyway?"

After the interview, the man thanked us politely and then went back to his corner and started screaming again.

AN ENCOUNTER WITH THE IRS
by Jerry Jones, SF '52

Coro really went through some tough times in the early days in San Francisco after the G.I Bill ran out. I remember the IRS man came around once and said, "You know, I really ought to close you down and put you in jail." I pointed out that no one was really getting hurt, and the IRS would get their money sooner or later. Coro was doing great work. He looked dubious, and suddenly I had an inspiration. I pulled out files of the current applicants, and the first one up was Craig McMicken's. The guy had done everything: president of his class, captain of the football team, Phi Beta Kappa, head of the debate team, and he had glowing work references. The IRS man read this application and said, "Wow, with that kind of talent, I guess you ought to stay open for another year."

SHOW AND TELL
by Bruce Corwin, LA '63

Like most young people, I came out of my college experience green and decidedly on the left side in my political thinking. I had zero experience with either business or labor or much of anything else. I remember that Don Fletcher took some of us out to meet potential funders as examples of what bright future leaders Coro was turning out. On one occasion, Don took some of us the Hillcrest Country Club to meet some prestigious people from the business community. In the "show and tell" segment, he asked me what I thought of business. I said, "I think that business people who spend all their time making money should give it away to community groups who are working for the good of the whole community." Don never turned a hair, but he told me later he wanted to put an apple on my head and shoot an arrow at it!"

SHADOWS BEHIND THE DOOR
by Ralph Cole, SF '47

As a member of the first Coro class of Interns, I was well aware that we were blazing a trail through new territory. Those were the days of Joe McCarthy and fierce anti-

Communism. To heighten the tension, Harry Bridges, head of the Longshoreman's Union and an avowed left-winger, was threatening to shut off shipping into the City. When some of us went down to intern with the San Francisco Labor Council, alarm signals went off in the financial community. What were these students up to? On the other hand, when the labor unions found out that there were Interns at I. Magnin's and Crocker Bank, they were equally suspicious that we might be spies. On occasion during seminars, we heard shuffling outside the door. When we sneaked up, then flung the door open, we saw shadowy figures disappearing down the hall. The feeling of being watched, of being almost certain that there were wire taps on our phones, lent more than a little excitement to being around the Pacific Building office. All of this made fund raising difficult and explains why Don Fletcher stressed that we should behave in a very professional manner. Coats, ties and hats were the required garb. We were always aware that we were pioneers in an experiment that might not last.

HAWAII TEACHERS LABS
by Jerry Jones, SF '52

One of the most successful tests of Coro methodology was changing the teaching of civics in Hawaii in the early sixties. The whole state of Hawaii is one school district and at that time the teachers were mostly Japanese females, and the principals were Japanese males. These teachers had not the least notion of civics. They just handed out books to students and gave a test at the end of year. The University of Hawaii contracted with Don Fletcher to train these teachers.

Don used a team-player approach. He divided the group into four different units, each with its assignment (identifiers, evaluators, summarizers, editors), and then the teams learned the Coro interview technique. Everyone had a role, and everyone was valued by the group. The progress of the students was astounding. They learned from the interview how to ask questions in appropriate terminology. At first, the teachers were shy when they interviewed a technical expert. "I don't know anything about this," they'd say. Then they learned to ask a question like: "Do you have enough people available to do the job being asked of you?" They learned how to ask generic questions and to get useful information.

They became self-confident and willing to depart from textbooks.

The interaction and drama galvanized the group. The results were dramatic. The teachers went back into their classrooms and changed the way they taught civics and social studies. The State Department of Education wrote into the curriculum guide a requirement that there be field work that is in effect to this day.

Don was somewhat of a puzzle to the Japanese since they tend to be very literal. I remember the first thing Don taught the group was how to practice a golf swing.

THE TOUGHEST FELLOWS

By John Greenwood, LA '68

I think we had the toughest Fellows group in 1970–71. There was a Vietnam war veteran who said, "I don't have emotions, I just have a hole where I used to have feelings." We had a kid who was homosexual and trying to come to grips with that. The Blacks and Hispanics were acting out. The women's issue was big. One woman in the program was a nun, and the first day of the program we met with a theater group who staged modern drama. After the program, she came to me and said, "If this is what the program is about, I'm going home." It was quite a group. But what is really interesting is that this is one of the few groups to have a reunion. Last year was the twenty year mark, and people came from all over the country to be there. There were ten out of twelve present. We agreed that we had learned more from that Coro year than any other year in our lives. I concluded that the happiness of the group at the time had nothing to do with what was learned.

BEST EXPERIENCE OF MY LIFE

by David Sibbet , LA '66
Executive Director SF, Trainer

I was a college editor, and went into Selection Day pretty cocky. I hadn't heard about Coro before and assumed it couldn't be very important. But it did sound interesting from a recruitment article Sid McCausland, a graduate, had inserted into the Occidental College newsletter. I

Wow, with that kind of talent, I guess you ought to stay open for another year. . . .

I.R.S. Auditor

Jeremy Jones, SF '52,
Executive Director, SF

had intended going into the journalism graduate program, but Coro selected me, so I postponed journalism. I was totally unprepared for walking into a little room over a theater in downtown LA, with windows open for lack of air conditioning and so much noise we could barely hear. I wasn't prepared for the assignment to study the "Logic of Culver City," starting immediately. I wasn't prepared for being grilled by a man named Fletcher who never answered questions, nor did I expect not to receive our Christmas stipend or never knowing in advance what was going to happen. I became massively critical. I didn't know what game they were playing, but through it all, I was pretty sure I was having the best experience of my life.

CORO'S SIGNIFICANCE

by David Sibbet, LA '66

When I joined the staff of Coro in 1969 and then became Director of the San Francisco office in 1972, my imagination was ablaze with trying to tell others about the power of the Coro program. I stretched for metaphors. Were we bees in the urban ecology, cross fertilizing? Or were we a kind of town plaza, a crossroads where things could happen freshly? Coro didn't belong to any one of the diverse elements of the city, but truly sat in the middle as a place for dialogue and coming together. I began to see that we very much miss this kind of open space in our public process and urban communities. In the public sector, we seem to have reached a point of "position paralysis". Everyone has a special interest, and there are few places where people can drop all contention and relate to each other as inquiring humans, talking about the richness and fullness of life, with questing, open minds. Coro, to me, was *a precious free zone*, a clearing in the forest, an urban Switzerland. I began to see why Coro had to remain neutral politically. As the years have passed, I have come to understand that living systems which become too rigid and disconnected die. Living systems, on the other hand, circulate, change, breathe, exchange

> If a man advances confidently in the direction of his dreams to live the life he has imagined, he will meet with a success unexpected in common hours.
>
> **Henry David Thoreau**

resources, and hold parades in the plaza. This is what Coro contributes to community, a place where community can grow in clearings.

Coro historically will be understood as a pioneer in education for *systems thinking*, although in its historical development, trainers did not use that terminology. However, the structure of its programs create an experiential matrix from which is it nearly impossible to emerge WITHOUT becoming a systems thinker. It is the only way to make sense out of the process. Systems thinking focuses on connections and relationships, seeing the wholeness that transcends the parts. The serial internships and regular seminars which help the fellows find patterns of understanding, supported by the conceptual frame of language of General Semantics, is the best hands-on construction kit for creating systems awareness that I know of.

Another aspect of Coro training that is quite contemporary, paralleling breakthroughs in quantum and chaos theory in the hard sciences was Fletcher's insistence that the curriculum be organic, almost self-organizing around the questions and inquiry of the fellows themselves. His refusal to write about the public sector or to codify processes was in fact an embrace of the higher order knowledge that emerges when human systems confront overwhelming new information and must jump through chaos to new levels of understanding and integration. This kind of process appears to be the hallmark of dynamic systems. Sometimes the greatest breakthroughs are achieved in the midst of what appears to be utter chaos in an organization—as occurred with Coro's crisis in the early 1970's.

Collectively, we Americans are experiencing change as furious as a forest fire. The old industrial order is dying, and new thinking, new relationships and new organizational forms are emerging. The process is confusing and frightening, just as forest fires terrify. But the heat is opening the seeds of new growth which cannot be discovered by forcing or planning. We must live it and experience it. These are the lessons of the new science. This is the brilliance of Coro.

CORO'S APPROACH TO COMPLEX ISSUES

By Marion Pulsifer, Orange County '84

We asked Marion Pulsifer, a 1984 graduate of the Orange County Leadership Program and an attorney with the California Department of Transportation, what difference her Coro training had made in her approach to solving problems.

I had many of the needed skills already, but I learned how to take myself out of my own situation and what I needed and to put myself into the other person's situation and ask myself, 'What do they need? How do I need to change in order to make it possible for this person to cooperate?' The ability to see the problem from another perspective and figure out what it will take to move the issue is the key thing.

Coro placed me in very flexible structures, so I had the freedom to innovate. For example, I had two weeks to determine the water policy of the building industry. I discovered they had no policy. So I found out what they did know; then I went to developers and found out what they knew. I brought together the interested parties, and they developed a water policy. Coro people create relationships which have not been operative before, help people discover a community of interests and the participants then can see new possibilities to solve problems. The potential for solutions always exists, but sometimes it takes a facilitator to enable people to drop their blinders.

I would say this kind of facilitation is the most needed resource of modern community life. We may know this, but Coro is one of the few training experiences which actually opens you to how it can be done.

A COMMENT

by Gene Siskel, LA '68

To this day I don't call Don Fletcher anything but "Mr. Fletcher," so high is my level of respect. Mr. Fletcher reminded me of my parents, who were activists. They'd see a problem, and with minds and hearts engaged,

A PERSPECTIVE ON CORO TRAINING

What got to me was the exposure to many different people. I identify more with people than organizations and functions. Yes, I learned how the system worked, but it was Harry Bridges who opened up my mind to labor unions, and Pat Brown who made politics come alive, and Paul Smith who got me interested in San Francisco as a city. I was fascinated by the different ways people thought, the different lenses they used to see the "same" event. Then I saw that was what the Interns did too, and I realized that was what I did. I was never quite the same after that.

Frank Aleshire, SF 1948

Frank Aleshire
1951

they'd do something. They'd give you their best advice as if they would be betraying their affection for you if they didn't. Mr. Fletcher knew how to reach out and tickle what needed to be scratched; he's a problem-solver. I was fresh out of college when I had my Coro experience; I didn't even know how to drive. Mr. Fletcher took me aside and told me I should learn. I did. I bought my car and drove myself from LA to Chicago after the internship. What a metaphor for what Coro did for me! It was there I learned to take charge and drive myself.

After Coro I had confidence that, somehow, I'd make it through.

ANECDOTES FROM SACRAMENTO GRADUATES

A group of Sacramento graduates got together in January, 1992, to share memories of Coro. Present were John Mockler (SF '63), Marlene Garcia (LA '82), Fred Taugher (LA '62), Krist Lane (SF '64), Ed Gerber (LA '60), Tom Hoeber (LA '65), Tom Dooley (SF '56), Maria Nicholas Kelly (LA '66), Frank Aleshire (SF '48), Jim Schoning (LA '66). Following are excerpts from their remarks.

* * *

As an agency hiring people in Sacramento, we always knew we didn't have to give Coro people the third degree because they had already had every kind of challenging experience you could imagine. The chief deputy in our agency knew about the selection process for Coro Fellows, and he understood the internship assignments and the reporting out process. He thought Coro prepared well; Coro people could "cut it."

* * *

I think what I liked about Coro was that I had come out of an academic setting where you were never challenged on an individual basis. You wrote your paper, passed the test, got your grade, and that was that. But in Coro you were thrown in with these twelve people who challenged every word out of your mouth. I wasn't ready for that, and it was upsetting. Still it was great training. It wasn't

just the diversity of your own assignment you had to deal with, but the diversity of the others' experiences, too. In a short time you get an accurate sense of how other people operate. It was your own experience times twelve. Mind-boggling!

* * *

My experience with Coro was that the staff went out of its way not to help us make sense out of anything.

(Reply) I felt that way at the time, too. I felt the trainers should be taken out and shot. But now I understand the wisdom of the strategy. Either they were so stupid, it turned out right, or they were onto an incredible methodology. What they did was say: "Yeah, well, what do you people think?" They didn't set up themes or try to structure what we should conclude. We ended up fighting a lot. So we learned from the group, but the staff was doing it right. Once in awhile you'd get one of those little papers that would say something like..." I notice when you talk you don't seem to hit on any fundamental essence..." Everyone got these little papers, and we concluded the trainers were some kind of aliens.

The diversity of our class was the big thing, not just racial, but age, gender, geography, etc. I remember trainers matching us up with classmates who were the ones you'd least like to spend time with, and then sending you off on an assignment together. In my case, a liberal Democrat to my toes, I got paired up with a conservative Republican. I went to public school, he went to private. We were a mis-match; we just didn't get along. I couldn't understand why the trainers didn't see this. Later, I realized that I had learned more from that person than anyone else in the class, and I wished I had been more able to hear what he had to say. I think this forced familiarity with ideas you resist is what sets Coro apart.

* * *

If you are negotiating a deal in a political atmosphere, Coro training has its positive and negative sides. You see, you instinctively understand the other guy's position, and this makes you play the game differently. You end up doing some strange things, from a partisan perspective, like slipping into compromise as a mode. You get so good at making deals you have to remind yourself of the value you swore to uphold.

(Reply) Yes, I sometimes find myself wanting to help an opponent to make things work right and proposing amendments when I should be closing the door.

(Reply) But, that's the value, isn't it? Coro says there is a process that should go forward, and there ought to be a negotiation stage. Public, democratic decision-making should include a process which recognizes diversity and accommodates differences and then negotiates all of this into a decision point. There has to be a process which allows give-and-take but which, finally, makes it possible to go forward. Isn't that the Coro value? To me, Coro says, "To the extent you can have all the parties participate in the process, you'll get good results."

Philosophy, Concepts, and Methodology

For human survival in the 21st century, society must develop a mode of symbolizing/philosophizing pertaining to governing and political dynamics which pervade all human activity.

Suzanne Langer

THE CORO CONCEPTUAL APPROACH TO EDUCATION IN THE ARENA OF PUBLIC AFFAIRS

This section of our book is a selective tour of Coro's backdrop of assumptions and philosophy. It touches on some of the consistently recognizable elements from which the training and experiences of the program participants sprang. Let's start by looking at Coro's purpose as expressed by WDF in a grant proposal to the Ford Foundation in 1962.

Coro's Mission

Coro Foundation was created to help bring greater sanity and meaning to our system of self-government and to combat irrationality, confusion and ignorance. Coro methods create attitudes and practices which will introduce a fresh stream of common sense and idealism into a jaded, cynical field. The inhibiting factors for this approach—which have made it difficult for present leadership to grasp it—is the dedication to ideology in the public sector. Successful business leaders in particular are more dedicated to trying to recreate old patterns of governance, ones they are familiar with, than trying to discover new and better ways to govern.

Fletcher, Ford Grant, 1962

It is clear from this citation, that the Founders did not choose to adopt a comprehensive philosophy, nor did they have an ideology to espouse. They observed that mankind has always been enraptured by various systems of thought but that political behavior, in particular, has not shown growth in sanity, rationality or humanity as a result.

As they conducted their "live" research in San Francisco and observed the repetitive patterns of behavior typical of the various organized groups, they began to search for more universal patterns that were not necessarily linked to occupation, political party or even cultural tradition. They became more and more interested in process, observing "what is going on" and less interested in examining causes.

John Dewey's classic *The Public and Its Problems* spoke to Coro's intent. Dewey advised against studying political philosophy and advised studying human activity to see if political behavior could be identified and described. "The facts of human behavior are accessible to human observation, "he wrote. Study the "how" and the "what" rather than searching for ultimate causes. Effects can be seen; causes are always hypothetical.

Dodge and Fletcher began the first Internship with an attitude of discovery. What was out there? What might the Interns see? Was there some training method which could clear the scales from their eyes and enable them to see clearly? How might their interpretive skills be improved? Could a discipline of scientific observation be introduced into the program? How could Interns, or Fellows as they are now called, be enticed into the reflective mode wherein they might think more deeply about what they were experiencing?

FOUNDER'S HYPOTHESES

The Founders did begin with some hypotheses. They were:

1. A universal political intelligence exists (people come equipped with skills necessary to relate to others and make known their needs);

2. Governing/responding is a basic dynamic which goes on at all levels of society whether in homes, unions, businesses, or government agencies.

3. A need exists for a formulated intellectual perception linking #1 and #2, and

4. A need exists for a mode of discovery by which people can THEMSELVES create that intellectual perception (rather than having it conveyed by text, indoctrination or legislative enactment).

From the beginning, Fletcher and Dodge turned decisively from the usual methods of citizenship training or academic political science education. Citizenship could not be taught as revealed truth (for who really understood it?) or transferred from one mind to another by inspired leadership or persuasive individuals. Citizenship, which has something to do with commitment, with one's skill in working with and relating to others, with one's identity and place in a group, was innate and universal, but often lies dormant. It must be brought forth midst experiences, lived and hungered for, and finally perceived and claimed in the individual mind. This process might never be fully understood. Citizenship "training" and leadership "training" as well would always have the quality of discovery as an individual and personal encounter.

As Fletcher and Dodge searched for materials to help establish the discipline of discovery, they kept coming back to John Dewey, Suzanne Langer, and Alfred North Whitehead and others. They also found Alfred Korzybski's scientific approach to language as expounded in *Science and Sanity* a core discipline to use in their training. But the richest discoveries of all came from the experiences of the Fellows out in the field. Each week the Fellows brought back reports of their activities, their observations. They shared their interpretations with their colleagues and were led to deeper reflection by the staff.

Even that was just the beginning. The activities of the Fellows created connections in the field. The field supervisors from all sectors of the community acted as models and mentors. Their observations, experiences and behaviors were fed back into the program. Some of the associations became quite close. For example, Jess Unruh, Speaker of the California Assembly, was taken with Coro and the highly motivated young people who showed up in his office from Coro. The highly successful method of coalition building practiced by Unruh became the subject for discussion in the Coro office.

Civic leaders who became Coro board members, who were interviewed by Fellows, who contributed their funds and trust to the Foundation also contributed their wealth of insights and knowledge.

Graduates of the program went out to become city managers, nonprofit executives, business managers, campaign managers, legislators, news reporters, mayors, volunteers, etc. They came back to be interviewed, to teach, to mentor and to serve. All of this enriched the environment for the current Fellows until Coro became a true learning organization, in process, always in a state of development.

Let us examine some of the prominent strands in Coro's approach to the community, to the environment which lies all around us, available continually for exploration.

> The map
> is not the territory;
> the word
> is not the thing.
>
> **Alfred Korzybski**

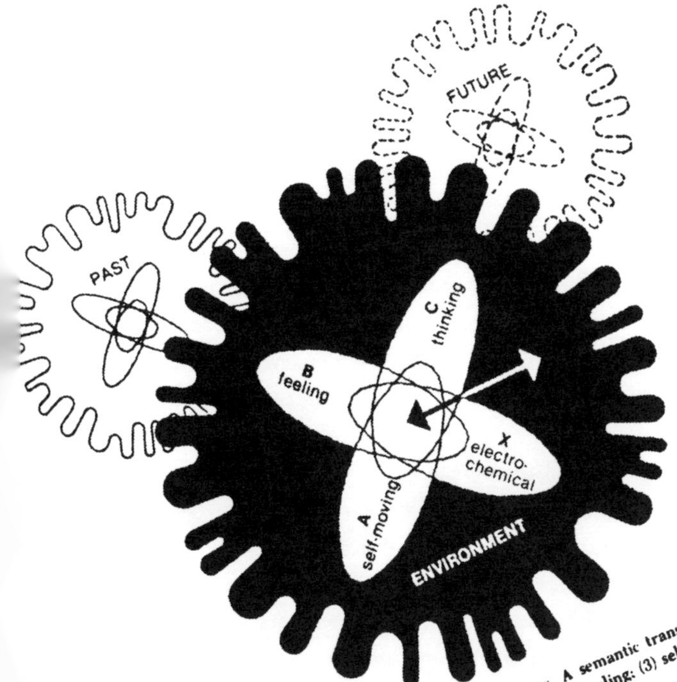

Figure 3.1. Individuals as semantic transactors. A semantic transaction has at least seven aspects or dimensions: (1) thinking; (2) feeling; (3) self-moving; (4) electrochem-ical; (5) environmental; (6) past; (7) future.

Semantic Transaction from Art of Awareness, Sam Bois, Wm. C. Brown Company, 1966

GENERAL SEMANTICS

How Do We Know What We Know?

People come into the Coro experience already loaded with theories, assumptions, judgments and preferred styles. Fellows especially have a huge stash of academic learning — which has anointed them with the certainty that they pretty much know what is going on. All of this creates a more or less impermeable membrane which resists or distorts new information. So the first challenge for Coro trainers is to pierce all of this and open trainees to fresh impressions. They must "unsee" before they can "see anew."

Fletcher and Dodge recognized that General Semantics could provide the shifts in definition and concepts to accomplish much of this purpose. General Semantics, or "GS," is a discipline which teaches us how we know what we know and increases our ability to manage ourselves, including our own thinking. An assumption is that there is not "out there" an objective world which can be satisfactorily defined. We humans create meaning, and each meaning is ultimately unique even though much (not all) of what we mean can be shared.

No attempt will be made here to explain all the theories of GS, but this book would not be complete without our attempting to put you in the place of a Coro Fellow, just opening up to a new way of experiencing the world and his colleagues.

Following is a sampling of the techniques which Coro makes available to trainees as they move toward higher stages of awareness and higher levels of competency. Alfred Korzybski's *Science and Sanity* is usually too much for most Fellows, but J. Samuel Bois' *The Art of Awareness* and S. I. Hayakawa's *Language in Action* have been part of many Friday seminars and Communication Weeks.

KEY CONCEPTS IN GS

WIGO (What is going on) Getting back to lower levels of abstraction gives us a better chance (better, not 100%) of making accurate observations.

THE MAP IS NOT THE TERRITORY

"Whatever you say it is, it is not." (Korzybski). " The map is not a map of the territory but a map of the mapper himself in interaction with the territory." (Bois).

ETC. represents what is left out (and something always is).

COW^1 is not COW^2 is not COW^3. No two things, beings, happenings are identical. EVENT^{1995} is not EVENT^{1985} is not EVENT^{1975}. This election may look like the election of 1992, but closer examination will no doubt show vastly more differences than similarities.

The Bois Model of Man as a Semantic Reactor

Sam Bois was a former priest turned management consultant who spent his life applying Korzybski in action, and translating his ideas to lay people. Bois' spirit helped Coro make GS its meta-model for talking about talking.

The diagram on the previous page is a cultural icon of GS. It challenges the idea that "man is a rational animal" alone, and instead suggests humans can be described as electrochemical (metabolism, activity of genes, etc.), self-moving (autonomic operations, muscle movement, etc.) feeling (drives, purposes, values, reactions, anxieties, etc.), and thinking (analyzing, conceptualizing, planning, writing, listening, communicating, etc.) These activities overlap, creating a single, integrated, complex organism.

Humans are affected by all the elements in their very complex environment: physical, cultural, social, psychological, professional, racial, national, etc.

Humans also must react in a time dimension, on the basis of what they remember from the past, what they anticipate in the future. Even though they can only act now, their interpretations of past and future impact them.

To say that humans are "rational," then is a gross oversimplification. Humans are "thinking, feeling, self-moving, electrochemical organism in continuous transaction with a space-time environment.

Bois felt human destiny was to constantly expand its area of freedom by improved thinking and/or expanding consciousness.

The J. Samuel Bois Model of the World in Which We Live

Between primitive humans and the unknown there was nothing but raw perceptions, wild imagination, fear and the urge to survive. Gradually, humans developed instruments of perception by which they could better understand their environment (circle 2). They also educated themselves into improved modes of thinking and behaving (circle 3) These better methods became fixed into theories, doctrines and symbolic experiences. A buffer zone was created to protect against the unknown and better manage the present experience (circle 4). General Semantics seeks to extend the system of conscious knowing by devising more scientific methods of knowing, disciplining and creating.

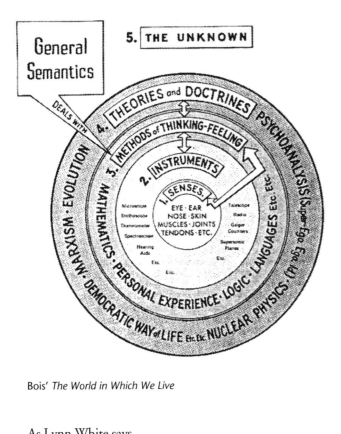

Bois' *The World in Which We Live*

As Lynn White says,

"We are learning to view mankind from vantage points other than the Acropolis."

Welcome to the Structural Differential!

Not long into the Coro experience, Fellows were introduced to Korzybski's "Structural Differential." A diagram of this model is on the next page. Aside from having an indecipherable name, this model was usually accompanied by a life model with cards and strings dangling and swaying from it, creating a memorable image which remains with most Fellows for their lifetime.

The Structural Differential provides a framework for understanding the ambiguities of language. Words which describe a "thing" are graphically displayed as being very far from the things themselves.

The "territory," or WIGO (what is going on) is a cosmic event represented by the parabola on top. Within this, human events occur when we abstract certain features of the whole and have a "first order experience."

Following this experience and our perceptions labels are attached at various levels of abstraction. Closest to our first order experience, we attach labels of description. Following that, we begin to interpret the meaning

BILL PEMBERTON, GS EXPERT & SEMANTOTHERAPIST

A large auditorium filled with students and interested passersby, there to learn about General Semantics from one of the world's eminent commentators, Dr. William Pemberton. Some Coro Fellows were tipped off by the Coro staff to be there. Small pieces of paper were passed out, which we touched with our tongues. It was then that we discovered that to some of us the taste was sweet and to some the taste was bitter: Eureka! People perceive the world differently, based on the most solid evidence. We were "getting into" the amazing revelations of General Semantics.

Bill Pemberton, consulting psychologist and practitioner of semantics and conflict resolution, worked with Coro staff and fellows over all the years of Coro's existence. He began his work in GS when he met Alfred Korzybski in Chicago in 1939 and contributed his expertise with projective testing to semantics research. In 1942 he was a presenter at a conference on GS at the Claremont Hotel in Berkeley where he met Don Fletcher and Van Duyn Dodge.

Because of his wit and his ability to make GS intelligible, Bill Pemberton became a favorite invitee to Fellows' seminars. He worked with Bill Whiteside, John Robinson and Diane Feinstein, even met with the Coro staff at a 1993 retreat at Ray Roeder's. Bill comments:

"Over the years the quality of Coro people has impressed me. My job has been to give the semantic orientation, the so-called philosophy and technology of Coro. I've been honored to be adjunct staff and hope they continue calling on me."

of the event, distancing ourselves from the event, abstracting certain characteristics and deleting others. Becoming even more abstract, we generalize, a process by which we equate one interpretation with another and make up general rules. These generalizations of course, are part of WIGO, hence the loop back.

The Structural Differential gave trainers a method to use in reminding Fellows that their interpretations might be some distance away from events themselves. The model became a useful tool to check the level of abstraction of a report or discussion.

After the study of General Semantics and levels of abstraction, Fellows understood more fully the reasons for trainers insisting that questions be carefully phrased to stay as close to descriptions as possible. The traditional reporter's questions of "who, what, when, where and how" became the 4WH tool, embodying this idea.

Human beings, throughout history, have shown themselves capable of reacting with passion to abstract labels such as: "communist," "American," "Jew," "alien." Fletcher and Dodge felt is was of critical importance that Fellows become consciously aware of how far from the territory they could stray when using language.

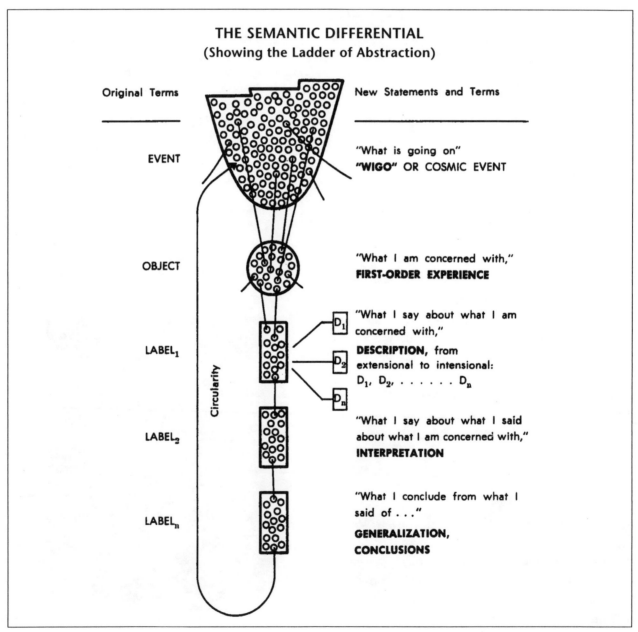

THE SEMANTIC DIFFERENTIAL
(Showing the Ladder of Abstraction)

Original Terms — New Statements and Terms

EVENT — "What is going on" **"WIGO" OR COSMIC EVENT**

OBJECT — "What I am concerned with," **FIRST-ORDER EXPERIENCE**

LABEL$_1$ — D_1 "What I say about what I am concerned with," **DESCRIPTION**, from extensional to intensional: $D_1, D_2, \ldots \ldots D_n$

D_2

D_n

LABEL$_2$ — "What I say about what I said about what I am concerned with," **INTERPRETATION**

LABEL$_n$ — "What I conclude from what I said of . . ." **GENERALIZATION, CONCLUSIONS**

Circularity

From Sam Bois, *Art of Awareness*

GS and Public Affairs

Coro understands that of all the arenas of public activity, the field of politics is the noisiest and most filled with illusion. Decisions are frequently made on the basis of belief systems which are very far from reality. These belief systems are often not held in common by citizens, so a constant struggle is under way for whose view of reality will prevail.

The political field is the place where interests compete for their share of the community's resources. It is a place of alliances where some are friends and some are foes. Campaigns generate passionate loyalties and real enemies.

In this heated arena the most noble sentiments are expressed, and whole publics are elevated by them. At the same time even virtuous men and women rationalize hedging the truth and excusing their own corruption.

Language both reflects and shapes political thinking. For some it's war. Contestants "campaign"; they "strategize and devise winning tactics"; they "out-maneuver" their opponents, and they "win or lose."

General Semantics, with its model of the structural differential, contributes the discipline which Coro uses to constantly bring the trainee from a world in which all are in some degree mesmerized by their inherited prejudices, fascination with the apt phrases, rush to simplify, fears, attractions to the personal, difficulties in thinking independently, and limited abilities to stand against the flood of emotional judgments, etc.

The trainee is cautioned to rely more on his/her first order experience to determine reality (what is going on) rather than on generalizations he brings to the experience. He is reminded to check the evidence, go back down the ladder of abstraction, delay judgment, seek corroboration, hold emotion in check, seek other opinions, practice non-judgmental listening, etc.

Paradoxically, the area of human affairs where people are most often absolutely sure they are right turns out to be the area most subject to error, with enormous consequences to the race. The 20th Century, in spite of all the traumas civilization has undergone, has turned out to be an age of renewed fanaticism. Coro's dedication to clear thinking is of central importance to education and to the health of our democratic processes.

S. I. HAYAKAWA, Ph. D.
Author, Language in Thought and Action; editor, ETC.: A Review of General Semantics; author of numerous scientific papers on semantics and related subjects. Lecturer, University College, University of Chicago. Past President, International Society for General Semantics. Dr. Hayakawa is a nationally known lecturer on general semantics and education.

J. S. A. BOIS, Ph. D.
Senior Partner, Bois & Howard, Industrial Psychologists, Montreal. Past President, Canadian Psychological Association and Fellow of the American Psychological Association. During the war, Dr. Bois was Lt. Col. i/c of Research & Information, N.D.H.Q., Ottawa. He has wide experience in general semantics, originating "General Semantics in Executive Management" and giving the summer 1950 training seminar at the Institute of General Semantics.

Turning and turning in the widening gyre,
The falcon cannot hear the falconer;
Things fall apart;
The center cannot hold;
Mere anarchy is loosed upon the world.
The blood-dimmed tide is loosed, and everywhere,
The ceremony of innocence is drowned.
The best lack all conviction while the worst,
Are full of passionate intensity.

W. B. Yeats, *The Second Coming*

JOHN DEWEY AND THE PUBLIC

John Dewey became known to classes of Coro Fellows through assigned readings. Although the first copyright of *The Public and Its Problems* was in 1927, Dewey demonstrated amazing prescience in predicting where flaws in the theory of democracy would lead to flaws in practice. He also saw that our political processes might not prove flexible enough to adapt to rapidly changing technologies and new social structures.

He pointed out that a sense of community, of shared understandings, underlies democratic self-governance and that this sense of community emerges from face to face contacts and negotiations within the body politic. These contacts have been broken in our modern society by rapidly changing technologies, by shifting residencies and by ever larger and more remote associations. The individual citizen has more access to information than ever before but has not gained an accompanying sense of power or affiliation. The citizen no longer feels connected to the community or to the state.

Even though we are in a new age of human relationships, deafened by talk shows, inundated with advice from pop psychologists, and urged to team-building in our offices, still, no political agencies expressive of the unity of citizen and state have emerged. "The democratic public is still largely inchoate and unorganized." (Dewey, p.109)

Dewey says furthermore that the real work of the state is carried on by trained specialists, so there is an

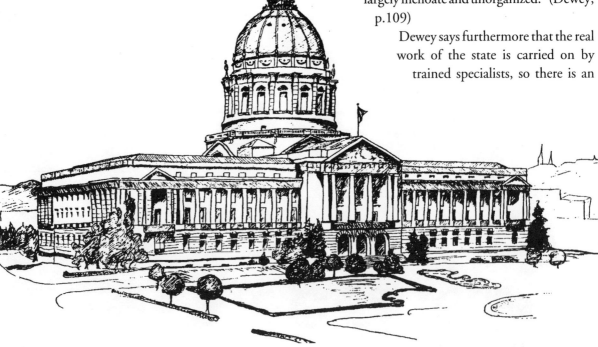

illusion of successful operation of government, but "the public and its organization for political ends is not only a ghost, but a ghost which walks and talks, and obscures, confuses and misleads governmental action in a disastrous way." (125) "Politics are carried on with a machinery and ideas formed in the past to deal with quite another sort of situation." (123)

What is The Public?

Dewey defined the public as: "...all those who are affected by the indirect consequences of transactions to such an extent that it is deemed necessary to have those consequences systematically cared for." (15) But today the "ramification of the issues before the public is so wide and intricate, the technical matters are so specialized, the details so many and so shifting, that the public cannot for any length of time identify and hold itself." (137)

Dewey even foresaw that the access of the public to more and more amusement would so occupy the mind of citizens that they would become less interested in public concerns. The mania for speed and motion would be reflected in a general restlessness and malcontent.

In the above paragraphs, Dewey spreads before us some of the central issues which occupied Dodge and Fletcher. They were devoted to the democratic state and to open inquiry, but they saw, too, that new processes, new disciplines were needed by the public in order for citizens to fulfill their vital role. The Coro founders saw that new links of connection must be forged between citizens and community.

Dewey also proposed some useful corrective action that took root in the thinking of Coro. He said: "What is needed to make direct and fruitful social inquiry is a method which proceeds on the basis of interrelations of observable acts and their consequences." (36) Dewey was a leader of the move toward experiential education. His ideas seemed especially pertinent in the field of politics.

Dewey saw the problem of democracy as lying in deeper social dimensions.

Community is Key

Dewey did not put his faith in modifying the forms of democracy, changing length of term in office, or populist reforms such as the of initiative and referendum. In his opinion such reforms did not go to the heart of the matter. Each panacea arises in response to a current need but then lingers to "cumber the political ground and obstruct progress." He saw the problem as lying in deeper social dynamics.

The citizen must feel, must be fully conscious of, his belonging to a community, to a whole greater than himself, which is responsive to him, which is part of him. "Wherever there is conjoint activity whose consequences are appreciated as good by all singular persons who take part in it, and where the realization of good is such as to effect an energetic desire and effort to sustain it in being just because it is a good shared by all, there is so far a community." (149)

Communication is central to creating such a community. Communication implies shared symbols, shared reflection and meaning, agreement upon goals and choices. In such a community there is rich opportunity to participate in groups which matter to the individual. These groups must function in such a way as to liberate the potential of the individual members.

How is such a community to come into being? Dewey said, not by abstractions and idealistic nostrums. Shout "Liberty, Equality, Fraternity" into the air loudly as you will, society will still go on crushing its members unless a behavioral discipline which values differences and open inquiry is adopted into practice by the citizens. He said we must go out into the community and there see what is taking place. It is there we must make adaptations and corrections.

One feels that Dewey would have been gratified to learn of Coro Fellows who went out into the field to observe and who learned the disciplines necessary to open themselves up to value the differences they heard expressed.

Dewey warned that we are not born into community. The young must be educated to value membership in the community, and they must be taught the necessary disciplines. The problem is essentially moral in that youth must learn to respect other members of the community. They must learn the art of give and take in communication dialogues and forebear impulsive violence. Education of youth should receive the highest priority in a democratic society since no other form of government is so dependent upon the self-discipline of the citizens and upon their love of community.

Requirements for the Greater Community

Dewey also warned that thinking tends to become habituated along certain patterns so that if citizens have only experience with their specialized professions, they will become unfitted to communicate with citizens from the general population. Thus civic life must always impel citizens to communicate with those who are not of their own occupation.

"Democracy is a name for a life of free and enriching communication," said Dewey (184) He lists these requirements for building the great community:

Insure freedom of social inquiry.
Widely distribute the findings of this inquiry.
Cross-fertilize disciplines.
Break through the language of specialization, use a common tongue, and simple phrases.
Provide for more reflection as to the meaning of news.
Encourage man's understanding of himself.
Go to the local community to build toward the Great Community.

The Coro program responds to all these admonitions. A diverse population of learners is brought together to share experiences, to reflect and to learn together. They are given disciplines of inquiry with great emphasis on language. The local community is used as the laboratory.

"We lie... in the lap of immense intelligence," wrote Dewey. "But that intelligence is dormant and its communications are broken, inarticulate and faint until it possesses the local community as its medium." (219)

> I believe in the beloved community, and in the spirit that makes it beloved, and in the fellowship of those who are in spirit, and deed its members. I see no such community as yet, but my rule in life is to act so as to hasten its coming.
>
> (Anon)

THE SCIENTIFIC APPROACH

by W. Donald Fletcher

Coro's premise is that the area of public affairs is complex, sensitive and involves interrelationships of personal, social and institutional factors which require some sort of scientific approach—the same discipline which has accompanied so much progress in other fields. No matter how chaotic the appearance, the assumption in the sciences is that there is some underlying order which will yield to systematic observation and correlation. Even if ultimate origins and causes may not be discovered, science has enabled us to navigate the field of the present with generally reasonable and even predictable results.

As citizens and leaders, we expend most of our energy promoting candidates and causes rather than improving the basic processes of governing and relating. So there has been no scientifically documented progress over decades of experience.

The Coro approach is to instill patterns of behavior and modes of thinking in order to enable the student to more adequately observe, interpret, conceptualize and participate. To bring about these changes in trainees, Coro:

1. Exposes the trainee to the field in action. He learns from the "doers."

2. Floods the trainee with new experiences, so he becomes familiar with and accepting of change.

3. Structures the trainee's opportunities so that he can experience the thrill of discovery and the satisfaction of personal mastery.

4. Leads the trainee to discover the "implicate" order, the order and balance which exist beneath the apparent chaos. Thus the trainee becomes dedicated to the system as a whole.

Coro's devotion to the "scientific approach" speaks to the as yet unfulfilled dream of the founders that Coro would place more emphasis and equal resources into the research part of its mission and not devote itself solely to training.

STRUCTURE AND FUNCTION

A quote which trainers and Fellows were very likely to find in their boxes with the note from WDF, "Be ready to discuss this relationship," was

Function produces structure, and structure modifies and determines function.

Charles M. Child

The concept was very important to Fletcher, and he kept returning to it. He explains it himself in a notation in his Liaison Citizen Journal:

Human patterns of directing, ordering, governing and relating are as old in man's history as the functioning of heart, stomach, brain, etc. We observe similar patterns, regardless of the culture. The hope for democratic self-government is that these patterns can be improved through training and education.

The role of Liaison Citizen (and Coro) training is to contribute to the inner thinking of all involved, not as partisans or busy bodies, but in a new role, enabling all to function easier and more as a single unit whereby governors and governed become one. Every real leader seeks to create that kind of relationship. The more often this occurs, the more secure our form of government.

"Why can't we all just get along?" asked Rodney King, a man violent in his opposition to "law and order" and yet sensing there must be something better. Fletcher speaks to that great dream, yearned over in the hearts of men and women from all sectors of society, the dream that sane, democratic self-government is possible. But we are imprisoned in certain structures, certain ways we have organized to get things done. The structure of bureaucracy, for example, appears to determine the behavior of the persons delimited by it. We are also imprisoned by the way we habitually function — by language, by habits, by assumptions we make about our natures and "how things ought to be." We are imprisoned by our history, our judgments and our reluctance to change.

Fletcher believed that all of these factors are learned patterns and that, ultimately, man is free to choose from a field of unlimited potentialities. By working on the process side, by changing his behaviors, his functioning, his ways of adapting to the flow of events, man can gradually change the whole structure of his community.

Functioning or behaving according to the demands of the task creates new structures, and these structures or organizational forms then modify how one can behave or function. If structure and function are interrelated, then as we change one construct, then movement is experienced in the other.

Modern Science

Today we would speak of paradigms which need to change, patterns of linked reactions in which one assumption reinforces another so that the whole structure seems unchangeable. Yet, democratic forms create processes which flow far more freely than in earlier tyrannical forms, so the pressure for change is incessant. Truly, we live in a tidal wave of change. All that we experience manifests what man himself is creating.

Fletcher even suggests that spiritual union can be achieved between the governors and governed so that all will unfold in a kind of felt unity. The training programs he and his partner, Dodge, initiated continue to work on this idea.

DEWEY'S PERSPECTIVE

By its very nature, a state is ever something to be scrutinized, investigated, searched for . . . It is not the business of political philosophy and science to determine what the state in general should or must be. What they may do is aid in creation of methods such that experimentation may go on less blindly, less at the mercy of accident, more intelligently, so that men may learn from their errors and profit by their successes. . . What is needed to direct and make fruitful inquiry is a method which proceeds on the basis of the interrelations of observable actions and their results.

John Dewey

CORO METHODOLOGY

This Section reviews the formal structure and function of Coro's programs, symbolized by the design of Coro's flagship program, the Coro Fellowship in Public Affairs, the nine-month, internship-based structure begun in the late 1940's.

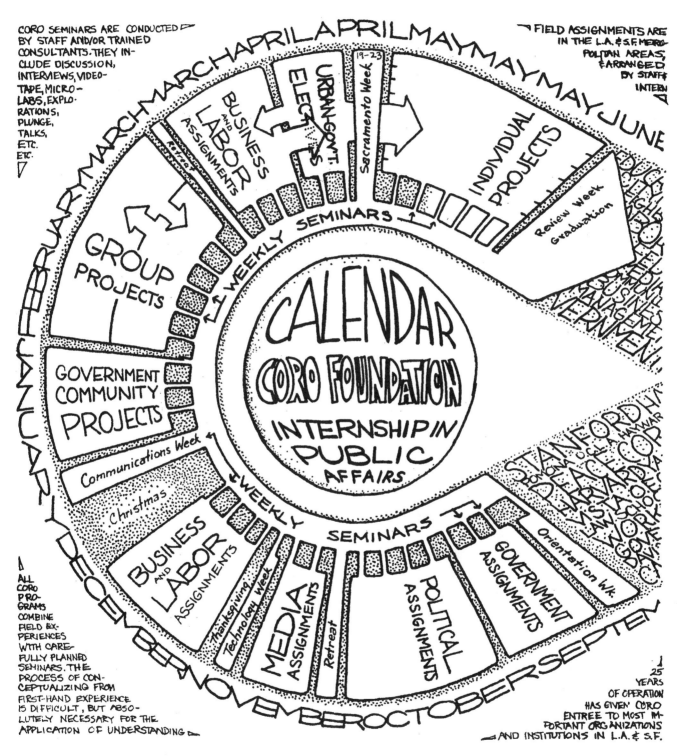

Program illustration
by David Sibbet, 1974

NATIONAL PROGRAM STANDARDS

In 1987, the Coro National Board of Governors decided that there should be some common standards which would characterize all Coro programs. With the expansion of the program across the country, the National Board recognized that the different Centers might adopt innovations which would so depart from the Coro design as to lead into another kind of training altogether. While not wanting to discourage creativity, the Board set out to determine whether there might be a core of Coro concepts and methodology which must be followed for a program to be "Coro."

Fran Aleshire, Ed. D. was retained to bring together all the Coro trainers at one three day meeting in San Francisco. Fran was to assist the trainers to identify those concepts, programs, methodologies and designs which identify a Coro training experience. This was done with representation from all the Centers, and then Fran wrote up the results and presented them to the National Board of Governors.

The Board adopted the program standards. In addition, minimal operational standards were also adopted. These standards specified that there should be at least one full time trainer for the Fellows Program; that the number of Fellows should continue to be twelve; that no more than twenty-four persons should be members of a Special Program, and that diversity of gender, age, political affiliation, racial/ethnic background, experience and geographic residence would be standard.

The Board concurred in supporting the original vision of the Founders. The Preamble to the National Standards reads:

A democratic system of government which is complex, fragmented, variable, and unsettled cannot be adequately described by a unified, comprehensive theory. Therefore, there is need for research and experimentation.

This system is dependent upon the development of citizens and leaders who are capable of governing themselves in such an environment. Therefore training for leadership in public affairs is an urgent concern of our democracy.

The mission of Coro training is: to strengthen our system of democratic self-governance.

The major goal of this training is: to train individuals who, as citizens and leaders, will all their lives act constructively and competently to build up and improve their communities and society as a whole.

The Board also adopted the outcomes on the following page as the desired results of Coro training.

Coro training is coherent and systematic. All parts flow from goal to outcome through the intermediaries of philosophical concept, methodology and activities.

Linking action with reflection is the most powerful learning model.

Cheryl Mobey

THE LOGIC OF CORO TRAINING

Mission: To strengthen our system of democratic self-governance.

Goal: To train individuals who, as citizens and leaders, will all their lives act constructively and competently to build up and improve their communities and society as a whole.

Philosophical Concepts
Public action begins with individual perception (Dewey); therefore, gaining the commitment of trainees/citizens is crucial to improving the democratic process of self-governance.

Methodology
The 4WH method of asking questions and getting information gives trainees a method which opens them up to receiving and integrating new data. Information gained this way is more likely to "stick" and to change the individual.

Activity: Internships
Internships immerse the individual in the crucial sector of the community where he can discover how things get done, observe power relationships, interconnections among sectors, etc., and thus grow in his understanding of governance. Having personal experience propels the individual toward interest and commitment to public affairs.

Outcome
Graduates makes a life-long commitment to public service.

CORO INTERNSHIP

Noting the success in the medical field of requiring graduates from medical school to spend several years "interning" in the field, the founders of Coro thought such a practice made sense in the political sphere also. Here, too, only limited knowledge could be transmitted in the classroom. The complexity of the subject, the variety of situations, the intensity of emotions, etc. called for observers to actually immerse themselves in the real-life situation and learn from practitioners. After all, isn't it an American tradition to learn political leadership on the job?

While this idea was innovative at that time, today there exist a number of "internships", some quite prestigious such as the White House Fellows. However, some of the characteristics of Coro's internships still are without imitation.

The Coro National Program Standards, adopted in 1989, have this to say about the internship portion of the program:

Fellows should experience five full internship assignments in the areas of community based organization, a corporation, a labor union, a government agency, a political campaign and/or trade association, media, and should have lesser exposure by other means to other sectors such as may be appropriate to time, place, or changes in society.

The founders wanted the Fellows to spend enough time in each environment to earn the trust of their mentors and to absorb the way of thinking and patterns of behavior which characterized that sector. Fletcher and Dodge early discovered that whereas the thinking within a sector such as business was quite cohesive, the thinking between sectors was definitely not. They wanted

---

OUTCOMES OF CORO TRAINING CLASSIFIED INTO SPHERES OF EMPHASIS

Intellectual/Knowledge/Thinking Sphere
An ability to:
- Demonstrate an awareness of language: role and constraints.
- Think critically: gather data, analyze, generalize, delay judgment, infer, evaluate, etc.
- Expand knowledge base by gathering data about issues, territories systems, cultures, etc.
- Think creatively and divergently from group.
- Use models, see and apply patterns to problems.
- See the thing as a whole: community, organism, organization etc.
- Apply General Semantics theory to explain how we know what we know: epistemology, perception.
- Understand structures, functions, relationships in organizations and communities.
Etc.

Political/Affective/Relationship Sphere
An ability to:
- Move people in a group toward decision.
- Negotiate, mediate, achieve consensus.
- Listen and to hear.
- Represent different constituencies.
- Be aware and evaluate the frames of reference of all parties to a transaction.
- Make a persuasive presentation by relating to the audience—seeing their perspective.
- Develop useful contacts and tie into networks.
- Use the senses, emotions, intuition to gather data: develop awareness as a whole organism.
Etc.

Task Management Sphere
An ability to:
- Allocate time, resources, personnel, funding to carry out a project.
- Plan a project, set goals, implement the plan with a group.
- Manage meetings from planning to implementation.
- Complete a project, as planned, within deadlines.
- Use a variety of reporting techniques convincingly.
- Work constructively with the group process.
- Reach a decision and act.
- Maintain communications with significant parties while carrying a task forward.
Etc.

Attitude/Values/Ethics Sphere
An ability to:
- *Make life-long commitment to constructive public service.*
- Seek personal growth, learning, new data/insight.
- Function flexibly with mind open to new input.
- Value collaborative efforts.
- Value diversity in its many aspects but also to see underlying wholeness (person and/or community).
- Take risks.
- Maintain a sense of personal identity and ethics.
- Manifest self-confidence and the will to act.
- Demonstrate a healthy respect for democratic processes.
- Demonstrate balance, humor, to "lighten up."
Etc.

Fellows to move comfortably in each sector, see the values of each, and identify common threads if there were any: this is the challenge of a democracy.

Fellows are Assigned to Management

Another innovation was that Fellows were assigned to the highest level of management. Whereas in other internship programs, interns are given work assignments and produce like any other employee, Coro Fellows were to shadow those who had real power of decision and who were usually the contact persons to government and other outside agencies. By this "helicopter" perspective, Fellows were able to see how their mentors mediated disputes, handled crises and organized their time. In many cases, internship supervisors took Fellows "under their wing" and gave them counsel and opportunities far beyond their original agreement. That so many busy executives have been willing to do this speaks highly about the quality of leadership in America.

The advantages of this type of educational program are obvious. The number of mentors, models and teachers is quickly multiplied. Even if the Coro trainer turns out not to be the best, or if one or more of the internship supervisors are not the best, the variety and multiplicity of assignments guarantees that the experience of the Fellow is incomparably rich.

Sector Experience is Mixed

There is another great advantage of this type of training over the classroom and that is the mixed environment. Learning about labor unions down on the waterfront, in the midst of the workers, attending union meetings, hearing the conversations, picking up the worries all add the sharp edge of reality to the educational experience. Then going to the corporate board room, learning about the risks of doing business, the uncertainty of profits, picking up the attitudes of business to the community... all of this opens up the Fellow's mind in another direction.

Coro trainers assume that human activity is expressed in economic, social, political, and religious realms. Therefore, the well educated person must become versed in the elements of each. As society changes and more functions are carried out by quasi-public institutions such as United Way, Art Leagues, youth organizations, crime prevention agencies, etc., Coro sends Fellows out to see how they do their service. The media has been added as a subject of study because of its powerful impact on public thought. Political campaigns and observation of legislative bodies are also recurring elements of training.

Another Coro characteristic in the program design is the opportunity to bring together the diverse experiences of the Fellows. Through the Logic Study, the group and individual projects, Communication Week and the weekly seminars, Coro urges the Fellows to share, to reflect and to connect up their observations and data.

All of this, with the Fellow always "in the midst" and "on the spot" creates a potent brew of never-to-be-forgotten experiences for the Fellow.

> From the beginning of his education, youth should experience the joy of discovery. The discovery which he has to make is that general ideas give an understanding of that stream of events which is his life. The understanding we want is an understanding of the insistent present.

Alfred North Whitehead

DIRECTIONS TO FELLOWS GOING INTO THE FIELD

We are interested in helping you gain access to environments from which you can understand the *recurring processes of public affairs*, and at the same time, develop *your personal ability to use these understandings* in the solution of whatever public problems you decide to tackle.

David Sibbet

Slim Delotto, 1951

FIELD WORK

Field world might be described as the "guts" of Coro training, where the rubber meets the road, and the Fellow finds out whether he can apply anything of what he has been learning in his seminars.

How will he be evaluated by his field supervisors? How will he gain acceptance in the organization? What is the nature of this new realm of his experience? What does he have to offer? Following are some glimpses taken from Coro documents.

Field work extends far beyond interaction with a few agencies. Weekly seminars are also included. These seminars will include guests, interviews, group exercises, analysis and synthesis of experiences, practice of communication skills and development of philosophy. Central throughout is the attempt to teach Fellows to test their own judgments and insights about public matters — as those events are occurring and in retrospect.

Field supervisors open doors for the Fellows, challenge facile interpretations, set up experiences. The Fellows will discover for themselves which elements are central and which are not. Those elements which they observe first-hand lodge deepest in their understanding.

(Guides for Field Supervisors)

WHY FIELD ASSIGNMENTS?

David Sibbet, Director of training in the early 1970s, writes

"The more an Intern's experience approximates the problem evaluating possibilities in actual work environments, the better. The Intern's purpose on assignments will be to develop as deep and as thorough an understanding of the central dynamics and concerns of an organization as he can in the assignment period. This process will be tested by fellow Interns who will be relying on him/her for an accurate summary and evaluation."

It was almost a given that Fellows were gifted learners and talkers. How would they fare as "doers?" The field experiences not only tested this aptitude, but they brought the Fellow to a new state of alertness, checking out a new environment, and figuring out how he/she might fit in.

A FELLOW COMMENTS ON HIS FIELD EXPERIENCES

by Drew Dougherty, LA '81

As a Dartmouth senior in 1980, hungry for the world of action and issues of real consequence, I decided to apply for the Coro program with only a vague knowledge that it involved varied, "hands on" internships. I arrived in Los Angeles and immediately was left with eleven other equally disoriented people in a hotel in a local community, Culver City. Our written instructions were to figure out the "logic" of Culver City. Four days later, we Coro Fellows presented our findings before the City Council and an audience of local leaders and media. It was with that shocking experience that I began to learn the lessons which today prove helpful in my job as press secretary for a Congressman in Washington.

The nine months in the Coro program amplifies the intense experience of the first week. One is confronted with the need to take a stand and answer for it publicly without the comfort of enough information or preparation. The demanding questions of public policy in the "real world", Coro's classroom, cannot be put off.

I found unique lessons in each of my internships. But whether it was my internship with the Los Angeles policeman's union which was fighting City Hall for the right to binding arbitration or with a State Assembly campaign in a painfully losing effort for reelection, I learned lessons common *to the effective movement of ideas in any environment.* I saw, felt, and tried out the intangible qualities, techniques, and styles which distinguish the effective leader.

The group of Fellows, too, who gather at least once a week to share their experiences, is the source of a great many lessons. A special trust, born of our shared frustrations and elations, allows for feedback and license to experiment with various personal leadership styles, a freedom often denied in the professional world. Ultimately, Coro teaches that answers lie within ourselves, not with teachers, books, "experts", or circumstances. Learning how to make the most of that knowledge is what Coro encourages. The diverse internships, which implicitly emphasize the interrelationships among the various sectors in the public arena, convince the graduate that truth is not the province of any one perspective.

OAKLAND OUTLOOK

Official Publication of Your Chamber of Commerce

OAKLAND, CALIFORNIA

VOL. II. NO. 9

NOVEMBER-DECEMBER, 1949

AT YOUR SERVICE! Presenting the Oakland Chamber of Commerce's new streamlined offices at 427 Thirteenth Street. New quarters

GETTING TO WHO YOU ARE: THE CORO GROUP INTERVIEW

Early on, Fletcher and Dodge discovered the power of the group interview. This strategy became the focus for the early laboratory courses and, today, is used in every special program. The Hawaiian project proved that teachers and students could use the group interview to learn civic responsibility. Fellows came to expect a group interview at their Friday seminars. Through thousands of interviews, Coro has perfected a powerful tool which arouses interest in self-government and teaches the skills of participation.

The Superiority of Personal Experience

Patrick White provides a good description of this part of the program:

"The interview captures the power of personal modeling. Our culture gives great weight to words as we educate each other. Yet we are all more influenced by contact with a great teacher. The teacher models a whole experience; words can never reveal more than a fraction of experience. The writer, with his linear words, engages in an endless struggle to say the unsayable, speak the truth which can only be revealed within an individual consciousness encountering a private experience. For these reasons, it makes sense to bring the learner into live contact with a person who has something to say, not just in words, but in his/her wholeness.

"We all know more than we can express in words. In the interview, the interviewee somehow manages to express that something extra. Consider, for example, the problem of describing to someone else a human face or perhaps someone you consider a great leader. How much more revealing the experience would be if you could bring the person himself to be seen, sensed, interviewed, integrated into the consciousness of the interviewers. For this reason, we rarely forget any group interview; there is a powerful, lasting impact.

"'What you are speaks so loudly, I cannot hear you.' We have an ability to take in a person's character, values, and attitudes when we are in an active presence. This exercise is primary with us and explains why we spend the first moments of listening to a speech trying to evaluate the credibility of the speaker —before we become engaged in his/her words. 'Who you are' always is a part of 'What you have to say.' A group interview

gives trainees an opportunity to attain and to practice skills/attitudes which will increase their ability to make accurate and useful evaluations as to the credibility of the interviewee—rather than getting 'stuck' on trivial impressions of how the person looks or his use of trigger words.

"The personality of the interviewee is amplified during the interview. Trainees 'get into' the essential person and usually find something of intense interest. The interview is compelling and involving and teaches the interviewers to focus with curiosity upon their fellow humans. The interviewed can become a model and actually change the course of a life—certainly, an attitude. Knowing how people resist change, this is surely a significant outcome.

Why is the world, which seems so near, so hard to get hold of?"

Teamwork

High team performance is a key objective of Coro training. The group interview is a potent tool. Trainees learn how to prepare and ask intelligent questions; they practice observing the responses of the interviewee; they are prodded to note every detail of the surroundings of the interview. Then, together, they piece together all the evidence, share their impressions, analyze their assumptions and reach a group consensus. They build their group pride by presenting their conclusions to respected evaluators.

Wanting to do well, the group assists and disciplines its own members, reaching for higher performance. People have a keen desire to participate at a high level, just as they do on the athletic field, and this is the inherent motivation that keeps everyone front and center.

Coro staff play the role of coaches rather than teachers, so they quickly toss the ball to the trainees, who are divided into teams. Each team has a different responsibility, typically involving the functions of asking skillful questions which identify the interviewee and what he does, and which, in some measure, evaluate how well he/she functions. One team might have the task of evaluating how the other teams are doing and giving feedback. At every step, trainees have to observe, think, participate, analyze, evaluate, plan, share and ultimately each individual submits his ideas/impressions to the rest of the group.

Balance

Coro is most interested in the political role because, in our society, it is the politician who must keep all the balls in the air, that is, he/she must be aware of all the interests involved in any given issue. He ignores them at his own risk. Therefore, training citizens means striving to achieve balance. Coro has many ways to achieve this goal, but certainly contact with diverse interviewees is among the most effective. Trainees come in burning with loaded questions to level at some "in the news" politician and often leave, completely disarmed, because "She wasn't anything like I thought she was."

Civility

Teamwork in a group interview calls for all the social amenities. Coro trainees are reminded to greet their guest, to properly introduce themselves, to ask questions with courtesy and to acknowledge the guest's contribution with gratitude. Respect for the other person and his/her right to see the world as he sees fit underlies our ability to govern ourselves. Trainees are requested to use simple, non-technical, respectful language.

Coro Tools

Every Coro participant in any program becomes familiar with 4WH and LDWpF. These acronyms stand for structural models which provide the unifying frame of reference for interviewers to follow. 4WH is the model used for identifying who the interviewee is, what he does, when he does it, and where he does it. A team asking questions can assign questions and evaluate their performance based on this model. These reportorial type questions help interviewers avoid loaded, long-winded, weak questions.

The LDWpF model is used more in an evaluative mode and to analyze the operations of an organization. Questions reveal whether the system which the interviewee operates within has an adequate DESIGN or structure, whether the WORKING PARTS (divisions, units, manpower, skills) can function within that design; whether there is enough FUEL (power, resources, motivation, values) to energize the operation. Finally, does the organization, its subdivisions, and its energy sources have enough assets to carry the LOAD (work, responsibility, burden, crises, pressures)?

> Every Coro participant in any program becomes familiar with 4WH and LDWpF. These acronyms stand for structural models which provide the unifying frame of reference for interviewers to follow.

With these tools, analysis can be carried to any degree of sophistication.

Age is No Object

Coro believes that any citizen, regardless of ethnicity, age, socioeconomic status, gender, experience, education, etc., can become an informed, constructive member of society. Don Fletcher's derivative program, Liaison Citizens, has demonstrated convincingly that youth is also not a barrier. In fact, young people are so intrigued by learning teamwork, by their contact with active leaders in society and their ability, finally, to ask adults questions rather than to be the ones questioned that they become expert interviewers. They are more willing to submit to the drill, the discipline, and they are more sensitive to the judgments of their peers than are adults.

This Coro strategy, the group interview, could profitably be introduced into public school civics classrooms and college leadership programs to redefine what citizenship is. Coro grads could promise lively sessions!

The Serendipity Factor

A great experience has a serendipity quality to it, a factor which cannot be logically defined or neatly expressed. Coro has always shown forth that mysterious, baffling characteristic. For this reason, we must approach slyly, by anecdote and metaphor.

"My Coro public assignment was with the LA City Fire Department," recounts Bruce Corwin (LA '63), and I worked closely with a captain who later became assistant chief. Twenty-five years later, Mayor Tom Bradley appointed me to the LA Fire Commission, and I still found my Coro contacts invaluable. Another connection grew from my labor assignment. I remember walking the picket line with the teamsters, in step with the union agent. Years later my own business was threatened with a strike. I called the same union agent

Could a greater miracle take place than for us to look through each other's eyes for an instant? We should live in all the ages, aye, in all the worlds of the ages. History, Poetry, Mythology! I know of no reading of another's experience so startling and informing as this would be.

H. D. Thoreau, *Walden*

and asked how to handle the situation. 'I can't talk now,' he said, 'call me at home later.'" I did, and the strike ended to everyone's satisfaction. This is an instance of how a young man's experience translated into something very important to my life as an adult."

David Abel (LA '69) will tell you of a series of incidents in which Coro provided key connections in his life. Wilmington was the site of his logic study; later he was granted the cable franchise in that city, based partly on his understanding of the city he was to serve. He interned with Jess Unruh, Speaker of the California Assembly. Unruh changed is whole concept of leadership in the public arena. Later, he worked on his gubernatorial race. "I came to appreciate labor unions by working with Mike Riley of the Teamsters and later with his son. One of my Coro classmates became mayor of Santa Monica, and I recently went to see another classmate, Jim Hunter, president of San Diego City College. When I was in law school, a guest lecturer was invited to tell us about the philanthropic work of the business community. He turned out to be Lloyd Dennis, chairman of the Coro board, and he reconnected me with Coro. Later he called to invite me to work for Coro. So Coro has threaded in and out of my life like the strands of a golden braid, always challenging, always leading in new directions."

Every Coro graduate could spin a similar tale. Young men and women are thrust unprepared and unsuspecting into adult worlds which turn out to be far more complex and provocative than they expected. These worlds then spin into other worlds, dissolve one into another, and connect across periods of time and interstices of space. People, events, experiences flow in and out of their lives and only years later do they pause to recall that all of this momentum got going when they became part of Coro training so many years ago. But it is hard to put into words!

THE BOTTOM LINE, HOW COME CORO WORKS?

Fifty years of experimentation in training citizens to participate effectively in democratic governance and to take leadership roles — that's the Coro record. What's the result? What is it that makes the training so powerful? What are the essential elements?

1. Firsthand, On The Spot, Personal Encounter With New Data.

We human beings are highly resistant to changing our minds about anything. We are used to seeing the world through familiar filters; changing any one of them might disturb others and be upsetting. The new data has to be jarring, irresistible and, above all, it has to capture our attention. This is most likely to happen if we experience the new situation ourselves. Hence, the most powerful element in Coro training is getting people out into the field.

2. The Challenge By Other Minds To Our Ideas And Personal Frames Of Reference, Our Paradigms, Our View Of The World.

Coro exposes the trainee to a new experience and then engages the trainee in discussion with others who saw/heard/experienced the "same thing." Only it does not turn out to be the same thing because for every "single" event there turns out to be twelve or more interpretations. Thus dawns the hard reality that what I see/hear/feel/ experience is a projection from within my mentality and not necessarily what is being seen/heard/felt/experienced by other mentalities. Implications are profound; priorities are switched from talking to listening, observing, sensing, etc.

3. The Experience Of Community, Of Connectiveness.

As the mind opens up and takes in new data, the trainees are more able to make connections. They "identify" with the people interviewed as humans with problems just like themselves. Seeing through the eyes of people from many different sectors of the community, they see how all the parts join up. They begin to view the community as a dynamic whole. They get the "big picture." They become "system thinkers," by instinct and preference, not by the book.

> Whatever the future has in store, one thing is certain. Unless communal life can be restored, the public cannot adequately resolve its most urgent problem: to find and identify itself.
>
> **Walter Lippman**

Coro Foundation
Model of the Program Year

David Sibbet

Chronology, Expansion, and Changes

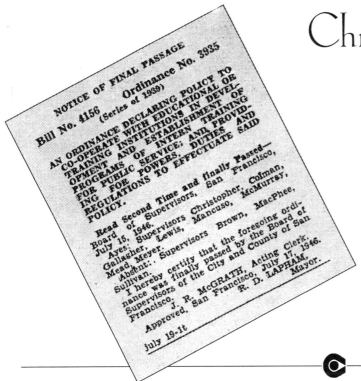

Some ideas sprout. Others die a-borning. Only a rare combination of circumstances can bring a great idea from conception to fruition. How such an event could occur is worth the telling.

In the manner of thoughtful Americans, Fletcher and Dodge pondered the state of American life and what might be required to improve it. The practice of democracy, in some respects, seemed little improved from the times of the Greeks, the intellectual base hardly advanced beyond the concepts of the Federalist papers.

They set out to find out: How come? The story is briefly told in this chapter.

Nothing would have come of all that inquiry had not many of their friends, their contemporaries, their students and then the next generation taken up the idea as a cause. Many others had to be inspired. Some young staff members took a decade out of their lives at critical times in their careers. Busy business executives put aside time and resources to lend a hand. Officials of labor unions were intrigued and put aside their reluctance to work with corporate America. Public officials and private officials took Fellows under their wings to shepherd them through their days. This story is also told in this chapter.

Finally, someone had to care enough to go into new territory, places where Coro was unknown, and there convince the people of those communities that Coro programs were worthy of their support. Some staff members had to leave the security of their known haunts and go into strange cities, hands outstretched for help. There they had to recruit among strangers and sell the ideas so long ago conceived by Fletcher and Dodge.

How they did this is also a story told in this chapter. This is not just the story of Coro; it is also the story of "how things work" in America. Ideas, relationships, trust, inspiration, persistence and lots of leg work and phone calls had to accompany this effort. Factor in the roles of public and private agencies, celebrities, our great, peculiarly American Foundations, the trustee attitude of some American corporations, but mostly, give credit to individuals who got caught up in the Coro idea and became willing to make personal sacrifice to advance it. These are the stories behind the stories, and this chapter tries to enlighten you on that score, too.

So now let us take you, chronologically, from the bare beginnings in San Francisco, birth and growing pains, to expansion of the Coro concept to Los Angeles, St. Louis, Kansas City and New York.

Can people govern themselves?

Stanford Laboratory Course, 1948

HISTORY OF CORO

The World of the '30s and '40s

At the time the founders of Coro were conferring together on what was needed to bring more sanity into the world of public affairs, the world appeared to be disintegrating in many ways. The peoples of this planet were struggling to emerge from a devastating economic depression. The USSR was deep into the Communist experiment. Germany and Italy were proclaiming the end of "spineless democratic forms of government" and had adopted "virile" authoritarian forms called Nazism and Fascism. War already raged in Europe as the democratic powers tried to hold back the totalitarian tide. In the Far East, too, a militaristic Japan was on the attack in China and Southeast Asia. Truly it appeared that the end of democracy was in sight. The initiative was all with vigorous, ruthless dictators. Critical questions were asked in America: Can people govern themselves? Can a free enterprise system provide enough jobs and fuel the economy? Can democracy arouse the kind of allegiance that the totalitarian systems seem to inspire? Why are people so displeased with the government they themselves have created?

Coro's Founders

W. Donald Fletcher and Van Duyn Dodge began having many discussions around these questions. Fletcher was a Stanford Law School graduate, 37 years old, and Dodge was an investment counselor, aged 45. They met during the Wilkie campaign. Fletcher was recruiting, and Dodge was helping write the economic positions. The two soon began having deeper discussions about the political process. Dodge was a student of General Semantics, and from that study, he surmised that the lack of sanity in political behavior had something to do with the structure of language and thinking patterns. Fletcher put aside his law career, and on January 14, 1941, they opened a small office in Mills Tower, San Francisco and began an independent study of the processes of citizenship and governance in the United States, and, specifically, in San Francisco. Five to ten friends met with them three times a month for intensive discussion and review of their research.

After a year, Garfield Shafer joined the discussion group. He had studied Jungian psychology in Europe, and he suggested that observation of group behavior might bring useful insights. Shafer soon began to systematically observe meetings of the Board of Supervisors, and he did, in fact, note repetitious and predictable behaviors among the legislators. And so the three men began to range beyond political theory and to study the behavioral sciences. They kept coming back to General Semantics, the work of Alfred Korzybski, where they found excellent models of how man symbolizes, makes and/or distorts meaning.

The Incorporation of Coro Foundation

On October 12, 1942, Fletcher and Dodge created Coro Foundation, incorporated as a public trust under the laws of California, with themselves as the original trustees . Dr. Edwin Cottrell, retired Stanford political science professor; George Hedley, professor, Mills College; and A.F. Mailloux, SF Building & Construction Trades Council were added later. The name, Coro, was chosen only because it had no connotations to confuse the public and because it had an appealing sound. The date, October 12, 1942, was significant because it was Columbus Day, a symbol of discovering a new world, and there was a play on the numerals: 1492.

Founding of the Internship

Dodge and Fletcher continued their research, interviewing in neighborhoods, observing legislative sessions and reviewing what they learned with friends. By 1945, they were convinced there was no existing organization which was concerned with the city's "spirit" and "integrity," and that training was needed for "more effective citizen involvement and more capable political leadership." They noted that there was no preparatory school or discipline for politicians similar to that existing for the fields of the law and medicine. But by now they were out of money. At this point Edwin Cottrell, Stanford professor, suggested a field program for political science majors. This became the laboratory course with students from Stanford, University of California, Berkeley, Mills College and the University of San Francisco sending students for Coro training one afternoon a week.

Late in 1945, Jean Witter, stock broker, and Dr. Cottrell pointed out that returning veterans would be excellent prospects for training and that the G.I. Bill could provide funding. In 1946, the City and County of San Francisco agreed to accept Interns from Coro, and

Can a free enterprise system provide enough jobs to fuel the economy?

John Johnson at Stanford Laboratory

the first Internship in Public Affairs began in January of 1947 with eleven veterans enrolled.

Why an Internship? Fletcher and Dodge were intrigued by the medical model wherein students had to experience an apprenticeship, working beside practitioners, before they could be entrusted with responsibility. This requirement seemed needed in public affairs where so much is done by "feel," where change is so constant, and where precedents seem lacking. They noted that in such training, the reputation of the Intern is "on the line"; he/she is responsible for results, and this reality arouses keen interest in the Intern.

Also, Fletcher and Dodge hypothesized that long term, enduring change in society arises from changes in individuals. They saw politicized movements creating short term excitement but usually being reversed and left behind in the wash of history. They saw political theories being passed around among intellectuals but not making connection in the minds of the public. They believed their best chance was to attract and train talented individuals and to trust that they would create positive change wherever they chose to spend their efforts.

From the beginning, the Foundation was supported by business, by labor and by government; the input of academia gradually decreased. The early program was experimental with all hands learning as they went. Interns were given field assignments in government, business, labor, associations, political campaigns, and on Fridays they gathered for seminars. Coro grew and prospered in San Francisco and developed a reputation for credibility and trustworthiness. Interns had an opportunity to observe at the highest levels, tagging along beside the chief executive of Crocker Bank, the editor of the Chronicle and Harry Bridges, the controversial chief of the Longshoreman's Union. The Interns became known as bright, positive young people, who could listen and learn, and who had an unusual understanding of how the community interfaced and solved problems, even in the face of apparent irreconcilable differences.

Although Fletcher and Dodge had developed a way to provide talented people for government service, they continued to play for higher stakes than that. They were using their experiences and those of the Interns to discover more about the way people govern themselves in a democracy. What works and what doesn't? How do powerless people gain power? What are the key variables? Are there laws governing the behavior of people in groups that take over? Are there blocks within human nature which work against the acceptance of diversity—so necessary in a democracy? Is there a "political intelligence" which any human being, of whatever age, ethnic allegiance, experience, etc., could use to resolve differences and make decisions? These questions touch on the "quest" of Coro, which provided the excitement in the program over the years while the organization was consistently producing leaders in every field of public affairs.

Expansion of the Program

Because of a grant of $250,000 received from Ford Foundation, Coro was able to open a Los Angeles office in 1957. Staff was hired and the first class graduated in 1959. The concept of "special programs" was developed, programs of shorter duration than the Internship, which often targeted specific populations such as senior citizens, ethnic groups, legislators, women, business executives, etc.

In 1960–63, Coro experimented with a laboratory course at the University of Hawaii. Jerry Jones remembers:

"The four years we worked with the Hawaii system were quite powerful. The entire state is one school district, so the changes that occurred spread through the whole district. The University was the primary teacher training college; the students were female because the male students were sent to the mainland for training in other careers. The women had no notion of civics and had been just handing out books for students to read. Don Fletcher's field assignments, his interview discipline, his question/answer model, his team development and his unusual behavior just galvanized the students. They'd never seen anything like it. The students made astonishing progress, and field work was adopted by the whole system and continues to this day."

Coro Graduates Gain Influence

Because of its research orientation and open minded ability to peer into the future, Coro has shown an uncanny ability to anticipate the direction in which the American democratic experiment was about to move. In the early days of the '50s, after WWII, this country needed trained people to manage the rapidly expanding urban centers. Coro produced city managers who were characterized not only by technical competence but who also demonstrated unusual ability to adapt to change and to communicate with citizens.

As the country moved into the '60s and '70s and the era of protests and assertion of minority rights, Coro graduates became more focused on political action. They worked in state legislatures, ran for city councils and worked for urban mayors. Every Speaker in the California Assembly since Jesse Unruh's era has leaned heavily on Coro trained staff. By 1984, fifty Coro graduates were working in state government.

The '60s and '70s also saw Americans more concerned about what was happening in the inner cities. Issues of homelessness, drug use, powerlessness of minorities, and chronic unemployment captured the attention of Coro people, and graduates soon were working as executive directors of community based organizations, counselors, lobbyists for these causes, etc. During the same period, participants in Coro programs became much more diverse with respect to gender and ethnicity. The *Interns* were renamed *Fellows* because "Fellows" was a more general term, avoided a medical connotation, and was associated with existing prestigious programs such as the White House Fellows.

Reorganization of Coro

In 1968, Robert Coate became President of the Coro Board, assuming fund raising responsibility. W.D. Fletcher became Chairman of the Board, retiring from his heavy, long term fund raising activities. Coro received a grant from Ford Foundation in 1970 to open an office in Pittsburgh and appointed William Whiteside, LA Director, to proceed to this city, with the assistance of Jim Schoning. However, because of the economic recession, this venture did not succeed, and the office was closed in the same year.

In 1971, heavy financial difficulties overwhelmed Coro. An audit revealed the Foundation to be deeply in debt. Key staff had to be let go in both northern and southern California. Bob Coate resigned to run for Lt. Governor and Jack Stieny, an electrical contractor and member of the Board, became President. Drastic measures were required. Founders and key staff were asked to forgive the debts of money owed, chiefly Fletcher, Dodge and Whiteside. Bob Coate made a critical loan of funds. Because of the generosity of these individuals,

FOUNDATION ADOPTS NEW DESIGN LOGO

(From 1970 Coro Reports)

The new Coro logo is the creation of Hisashi Nakamoto, senior art director of Hoefer, Dieterich & Brown, Inc., a San Francisco advertising firm.

A logo, like a name, becomes a symbol of the organization it represents, Nakamoto said. Unlike Coro's name, which is a coined word into which the foundation built its own meaning, the new logo initially evokes certain concepts Nakamoto felt were central to Coro's endeavors.

"I began with a dome, then the letter 'C'," Nakamoto said. "Some had arrows and an 'F' inside, others had circles. After 20 designs and a lot of discussion about the foundation, the more appropriate the simple 'C' and circle seemed."

"The center part of the 'C' is meant to look like an eye to represent the fact that Coro always has its eyes open in public affairs. It is also in the center. I always think of a center as being strong, a foundation."

"Yet in spite of being strong and in the center, there is still an opening. Coro is always an open thing. It also seems to be pointing out in a direction," Nakamoto said.

Nakamoto is pleased that the logo has ended up representing many different things.

James C. Nelson, Jr., vice president of Hoefer, Dieterich & Brown, Inc. and trustee of the Coro Foundation, arranged for the donation of the new logo.

Coro was able to shake itself and move on. Also, by fortuitous circumstance, a process had been set in motion several years before to change Coro to a non-profit corporation from a public trust, so this new vehicle could be used to create a Coro Foundation free of all but immediate debts. David Sibbet became Executive Director in San Francisco and John Greenwood assumed the same position in Los Angeles.

Coro Creates New Centers

Several lucky breaks occurred to help the new organization. In 1972, the Danforth Foundation sought out Coro and gave it funds to open an office in St. Louis. This project moved forward rapidly with Jim Schoning, Don Kornblet, and Alex Hartley playing key leadership roles. They were trained in the Los Angeles office, which provided staff support during this critical time; they then moved to St Louis to launch the first program.

In San Francisco, Sibbet crafted a grant for the San Francisco foundation to reorganize the operations of Coro as a multi-program "Center", and received a three year grant for operations, thereby launching the Centers idea.

With the expansion of Coro to other sites, the Foundation saw a need for a national center, so the National Board of Governors was created. This Board had a chair, representatives from the Centers and some at-large members. The hope was that Coro would assume a national identity and begin to define the common threads of all Coro programs. The relationship between the National Board and the Centers remained to be defined.

Fletcher Creates Liaison Citizens

During this period, W.D. Fletcher resigned from the Coro Board to devote his full attention to his new program, Liaison Citizens. With this move, Fletcher returned to his original research to determine whether citizens of any age, ethnicity or level of experience could work together to become self-governing citizens and to create livable communities. He opened an office in East Los Angeles, one of the most under-served and poorest sections of the city and proceeded to live a Spartan life, bringing his dream to reality.

In 1975, both David Sibbet and John Greenwood traded their Executive Director roles for that of Directors of Training, believing that the long term health of

the organization rested on the quality of its programs and that this goal required the attention of the most senior level people possible.

Growth Resumes

In 1973 Richard Butrick was named Executive Director in San Francisco and Mike Roos, followed by Jack Flanagan became Directors in Los Angeles. Staff teams launched a host of special programs that soon brought Coro back to financial health. During this period, Coro began the Women's Program, the Businessmen's Public Affairs Program, the African American Leadership Program, Inservice training for teachers, Freshman Orientation to the California Legislature, and also began sending out the Corospondent.

Van Duyn Dodge, who had been ailing for several years, died in 1975, leaving a very large gap in Coro's leadership. In 1976, an office was opened in Kansas City which, from then until now, offered a summer Fellows program. A Coro Center was opened in New York in 1979 with the encouragement of the National Board of Governors and assistance from local graduates. Jim Schoning was sent East to help the Center get started, and Mary Ellen Irwin got the recruiting off the ground. Karin Eisele became Director in 1982. The first Fellowship was offered in 1984.

The National Board of Governors appointed Dr. John McClosky of St. Louis as the first national director of Coro. McClosky was a professor of political science and Director of the St. Louis Center. The need was seen for a unifying, distinguished head of Coro who would provide the leadership formerly given by W.D. Fletcher. However, the idea floundered, possibly because of failure to think through the relationship between the national head and the Centers, particularly in the touchy area of funding. National leadership returned to the Chairperson of the National Board. The Board sets national program standards, assists Centers when necessary, explores the start up of new centers, receives national funding, encourages meetings of Center staffs and acts generally to facilitate coordination and communication among Centers.

Coro Today

Today Coro is governed by a National Board and by local Boards of Directors in the four Centers: San Francisco, Los Angeles, Midwest (St. Louis) and New

York. Each Center is separately incorporated but is also affiliated with the National. In addition, the Kansas City office has a Board of Directors and sets policy for its own program. Each Center has an Executive Director, a Director of Training and support staff. Training is also done by volunteers in each community: managers in diverse industries supervise and advise Fellows, and hundreds of busy public and private officials offer themselves as interviewees and mentors for Coro Fellows. List of donors to support Coro read like Who's Who in each community.

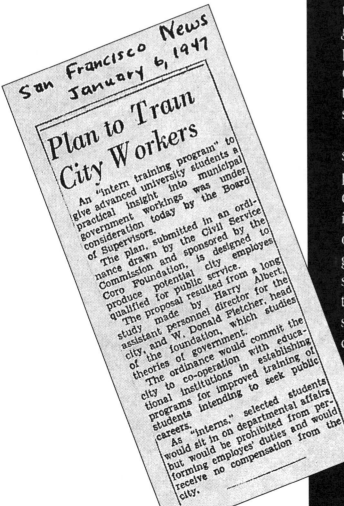

San Francisco News
January 6, 1947

Plan to Train City Workers

An "intern training program" to give advanced university students a practical insight into municipal government workings was under consideration today by the Board of Supervisors.

The plan, submitted in an ordinance drawn by the Civil Service Commission and sponsored by the Coro Foundation, is designed to produce potential city employes qualified for public service.

The proposal resulted from a long study made by Harry Albert, assistant personnel director for the city, and W. Donald Fletcher, head of the foundation, which studies theories of government.

The ordinance would commit the city to co-operation with educational institutions in establishing programs for improved training of students intending to seek public careers.

As "interns," selected students would sit in on departmental affairs but would be prohibited from performing employes' duties and would receive no compensation from the city.

THE CORO MISSION

Developing future leaders and strengthening communities is what Coro is all about.

For 50 years since its founding, Coro has operated on the basic premise that the survival of a *democratic form of government* depends on the participation of individuals who are not only committed, but who are competent to administer the system and to strengthen and protect its basic tenets.

The development of leaders in our society is a complex process, particularly now with the enormity of change that has occurred, and most important, with the increasing diversity of our population. Americans take for granted that the process will work successfully for each generation. Today, too much is at stake to leave the future simply to chance. And this is where Coro can make a difference.

THE AMAZING G.I. BILL

Coro was one of the unexpected triumphs of the G.I. Bill. Casting about for some way to finance their new educational ideas, Fletcher and Dodge were alerted to the possibilities of the G.I. Bill by Professor Edwin Cottrell of Stanford. They learned that returning veterans would receive tuition and a living allowance for their period of military service. They could apply their credits to a Coro Internship.

Public Law 346, the Service Man's Readjustment Act of 1944, turned out to be one of the most important laws ever passed, but the results were largely unexpected. Congress knew they had to do something to keep the masses of returning veterans "off the streets," but the idea that so many of these young men would choose to go to college never occurred to them. They thought the unemployment allowance would be more used. Only through the frantic last minute lobbying of the American Legion was the bill passed. The servicemen came from a Depression era. Many were from small towns where half of the young men dropped out of school and went to work. The idea that most young Americans should aim for college was an unthought of idea. The veterans who, on their own initiative, began streaming to college campuses were the first in their families to have such dreams. Of the 14 million men eligible, 2.2 million jumped at the chance to earn a college degree.

The G.I. Bill pulled a generation of the poor, of immigrants, of blue-collar workers up by their combat bootstraps and put them among the best educated, most affluent of generations in history. They broke the manual labor chain of employment and put college within reach of millions, not only for themselves, but for all succeeding generations. The first bill, which cost $5.5 billion, turned out 450,000 engineers, 240,000 accountants, 91,000 scientists, 238,000 teachers, 22,000 dentists and thousands of other professionals. Graduate degrees also became possible; a whole new level of expectation opened for millions of Americans.

The Bill also revitalized colleges. $500/year was paid per veteran for tuition and $75/month for subsistence. Enrollments skyrocketed; classrooms were jammed. Lights burned from dawn to dusk, for the veterans turned out to be superior students. Old myths were blown away. They raised the grade point averages at Stanford, Princeton and Harvard as well as at public universities. Fathers were the best students of all.

Some professors were taken aback by the searching questions asked by these veterans of the Battle of the Bulge, island invasions and naval actions, but educators like Fletcher and Dodge relished the honesty and simplicity of these youths. They just fit the Coro approach, and they got the Internship off on a firm foundation, rooted in questioning and experience and tolerance for risk.

12 VETS LEARN HOW TO RUN CITY

City Hall Training Starts This Week Under Scholarships

A San Francisco foundation devoted to developing understanding of municipal administration is blazing a new path in student training for public office.

It announced the award of nine months "interneship" in city and county offices to twelve war veterans who plan careers as public officials.

Donor of the scholarships was the Coro Foundation, of 821 Market Street. Each is for $900.

U.C. STUDENTS

Eight of the winners are University of California students. Two are from Stanford University and the remaining two live in San Francisco, the foundation said.

Only woman picked for the unusual honor was Miss Alice M. Reynolds, a former WAVE now studying at U.C. Other winners: San Francisco, Thomas C. Fleming; Oakland, Harold J. Chase, David E. Nelson and Robert A. Popp; Berkeley, Mobley M. Milam and Thomas Sullivan; San Jose, Ralph N. Cole and John J. Johnson, and John E. DeVito, Martinez; Richard L. Cromartie, San Mateo, and Robert T. Mautner, Los Angeles.

NEW INTERNES

The new internes will begin their training this week in the City Hall, rotating among several offices for about eight weeks before settling down in one department for more intensive study.

First Class, 1947

CHRONOLOGY

1940

Dodge and Fletcher met each other while working on the Willkie campaign. December of that year, WDF attended a General Semantics seminar at the urging of Dodge.

1941

Curtis O'Sullivan, manager of the Mills estate, offered the pair a rent-free office in the Mills Tower. Dodge said, "Let's see if we can come up with a few ideas."

1941–45

Research period consisted of:
1) Talking to people of diverse backgrounds;
2) Attending Board of Supervisor meetings;
3) Door to door interviews with citizens in neighborhoods (precursor to Logic Study).
4) Evening meetings with friends to discuss what they were observing, thinking, learning.

By April, 1941, they were assisted by volunteers. They were reading John Dewey, *The Public and Its Problems* and Alfred Korzybski, *Science and Sanity*. They came across an organizing principle, that language largely determines society's interpretations and affects cultural sanity.

The Pacific Building, 821 Market Street, SF

1942

February, this year, Garfield Shafer joined them and began to observe the Bd/Supervisors. He developed a chart which showed interactions were predictable.

October of this year, they created a public trust to conduct research into the public process. They chose Columbus Day as symbolic of their quest; 1492 had the same numerals. At this point WDF was 34, Dodge was 44.

The name Coro was coined precisely because it had no connotations, and the sound was appealing. "Foundation" was added until 1991 when it was dropped because it implied Coro was a philanthropic organization.

1943–44

WDF and Dodge considered what Coro might do. They found no organization concerned with the city's *spirit and integrity*. The large community needed a communication linkage/process such as exists in small cities, and it needed "more effective citizen involvement and more capable political leadership."

1945

Funding was needed. Edwin Cottrell, professor of political science at Stanford, suggested a field program for poli sci majors, one afternoon a week in SF. This became the laboratory course in public affairs, which was a staple of Coro's for many years. Participating colleges were Stanford, Mills, Cal Berkeley, University of San Francisco. Coro moves to Pacific Building.

November 1945

Jean Witter and Dr. Cottrell suggested that returning veterans would be excellent students and that they could be funded by the G.I. Bill of Rights. The Internship Program was born.

1946

The City/County of San Francisco agreed to cooperate with Coro and help train students, called "Interns".

1947

The first Internship began with eleven veterans. A Coro Board of top business, labor and government executives was recruited for advice and support. The program was experiential, not academic, with WDF and Dodge learning and adapting as they went. Interns were given field assignments in government, business, labor, public agencies. Political campaigns were not added until 1953. Fridays, Interns gathered for seminars. Hal Chase, Dick Cromartie, and John Johnson were the first trainers, followed by Frank Aleshire, Bill Dillinger, Ed Benson, all newly graduated Interns. Prestigious friends supporters such as Dr. Bill Pemberton, Professor George Hedley, Dr. Edwin Cottrell and Julius Jacobs helped out.

Early '50's

Sam Sewall (SF '49) was a trainer from 1950–1956. Dorothy Schell Hudgins, also '49, was a special assistant to WDF and worked to develop theory and methodology.

1955–63

A grant ($285,000) was received from Ford Foundation to open a Los Angeles office. Staff, hired in 1956, was Austin

Woodward, Director; Bill Whiteside, Mary Kehew, trainers. The first class graduated in 1959. Pilot programs were begun in both SF and LA to experiment with different training forms and student populations.

An internship type program was run with Occidental College to develop a Master's Degree in urban policy. Mary Kehew was principal LA trainer from 1959–1969. In 1960–63, Coro experimented with a laboratory course at the University of Hawaii—which was continued by the University after Coro's departure. A program was conducted for Koreans through the Asian Foundation, pioneering special programs for the ethnically diverse. A

Ruth James, all around assistant

John R. Johnson, Early Staff

Both Business, Labor Support Coro Work

By Jack Miller

The Coro Foundation, the off-spring of a series of bull sessions held by prominent San Franciscans before the war, "is very much a success."

This opinion was expressed here today by W. Donald Fletcher, director and a co-founder of the non-profit organization set up to develop leaders for public affairs.

Mr. Fletcher, an attorney who hasn't practiced law since the Coro bug bit him in 1940 "testimoni..."

Foundation trains for public life

_____ _____ South

In time, he predicted, the program will be operating "on a much bigger basis." Already, the foundation is working to establish an office in Los Angeles. The "response has been very cordial" in the South and "in the near future" he thinks the foundation should be in business there.

"We have had to turn applicants away for the Coro Foundation," Van Duyn A. Dodge, a co-founder and chairman of the foundation's board of trustees, declared in emphasizing the way the "idea" has taken hold.

Dodge, a partner in the securities firm of Dodge & Cox here, "spends a good many hours each week" in behalf of the Coro Foundation.

"There's no other program like it anywhere else in the country," he declared in an interview at Coro's headquarters in the Pacific Building, 821 Market-st.

Both Mr. Dodge and Mr. Fletcher today recalled the many bull sessions they had with groups of San Francisco business and profession people to see what could be done about building up leaders for important posts in public life. That was in 1940.

Lots of Talk

After 18 months of talk and investigation, the Coro Foundation was establi___
Fletcher ____
more ye___
education ____

A laboratory course, to supplement undergraduate class work in Bay Area colleges, was introduced in 1945. Two years later the foundation's main mission, the Internship in Public Affairs, was born.

The internship, designed for college graduates interested in public careers, is a nine-month training program. Interns not only get a chance to learn firsthand how the government operates, but also business and labor.

Twelve "highly selected" grad-

uates go through the Coro internship program each year. They get a subsistence scholarship of $1000 plus an additional amount according to the number of dependents they have.

"Basically, it's boot camp training for public life," the Coro people explain.

Jeremy Jones, a 1952 product of the Coro Foundation and now on its staff, puts it this w___
"The f___ ___ ___
___ ___ interplay between business interests, labor and government. So we try to give an intern experience in all these fields."

General Support

The Coro Foundation, which operates on a modest $50,000 a year budget (and that includes everything), is one subject on which business and labor don't quibble. Each gives the foundation financial support and co-operates in its training program, Mr. Jones emphasized.

Although the average age of the graduate Coro intern now is about 30, some 60 per cent of them already hold administrative or management positions.

About 58 per cent of them are in public service, ___ ___ business, 3 per ___ ___ (a difficult field ___ from out of the r___ per cent in journali___ tion. Law gets 5 per___

Since only a bit m___ of the foundation's ___ ___ ___ into government, ___ ___ appoint the organ___

Not by any me___ indicated.

Show in___

"Our hope is ___ will wind up s___ they can exert ___ public affairs.

"We are not looking for them to set the world on fir___ first ___

___ ___ ___ Coro graduates will work up to responsible positions in the community in whatever field they are in."

A citizenship program, for elementary and high school teachers, also is conducted by the foundation at San Jose State College in the summer. It aims to teach the teac___ what actually g___ community so th___ do a better teac___

What does the ___ mean?

Nothing in p___ Jones explained. ___ pulled out of the ___

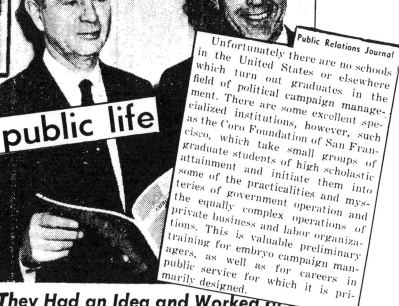

Public Relations Journal

Unfortunately there are no schools in the United States or elsewhere which turn out graduates in the field of political campaign management. There are some excellent specialized institutions, however, such as the Coro Foundation of San Francisco, which take small groups of graduate students of high scholastic attainment and initiate them into some of the practicalities and mysteries of government operation and the equally complex operations of private business and labor organizations. This is valuable preliminary training for embryo campaign managers, as well as for careers in public service for which it is primarily designed.

They Had an Idea and Worked at It

Van Duyn A. Dodge, left, chairman of the Coro Foundation's board of trustees, looks over the Coro record with W. Donald Fletcher, director. They are co-founders of the "leader development" organization.

Coro Foundation Trains Students For Government, Business, Labor

THE GOAL of Coro foundation is to insure the more intelligent handling of public affairs. Each year 12 men and women from all parts of the country are selected as "interns" for a nine months' training program running from Octobe___ through June.

Coro Finds New Leaders

CORO FOUNDATION, the nonprofit public trust which each year gives a dozen highly selected men and women an internship in public affairs, is now entering its tenth year of service in San Francisco.

The Foundation ___ recruiti___ ___ from the community in ___ ___ ___ candidates obtainable for ___ ___ ___ subsistence scholarships ___ ___ full-time activity are provided, with ___ purpose of giving the trainees first-hand knowledge of government, business, labor and politics as they pertain to the training of persons for public affairs.

Past Coro teams have done important jobs for the community: for example, the survey of San Francisco's mental health problem and the study of San Francisco's traffic situation.

Internship gives practical training

Labor Council renews its backing of Coro Foundation

Labor's endorsement of the work of Coro Foundation was renewed last week by the San ___ ___

tor of the Building Service Employees, and Al Maillouz, building trades business representatives, currently serve on the Foun-tives, ___ ___ Trustees. Con-

'Novice' Politician Gets Top Cal. Post

Libby Smith Rises Fast With Demos

By Mary Ellen Leary

Probably no one ever had so extraordinary an introduction to politics as Libby Smith.

Six year ago she didn't know a party committeeman from the milk man. And she knew far more about the cost of a dinner party than the cost of a congressional campaign.

There was one valuable schooling which helped her in politics: Coro Foundation.

from the East after the war because her husband, shippin[g] ‸ough, had fallen in lov[e] ‸th the Bay and the hills.

Never Dreamed Politic[s]

She'd gone through warti[me] crowded housing with teen-age daughter and young son, endured the s[hock] when war left her Navy ‸cer husband battle-deaf[,] now uses a hearing aid[,] helped him through the[m] into a successful new b[usiness] career in San Francisco.

She had been a Grey [Lady,] a Red Cross board m[ember,] even a Junior League[r,] joined the World Affai[rs Coun-] cil, cared about sch[ool,] worked for their imp[rovement] in Marin.

But politics—? S[he] d[...]

s[...] ha[...] P[...]

DAILY PALO A[LTO]

Aiassa Takes Reins As New City Chief

Puente Selects City Manager From Field of 8

PUENTE — Franklin D Aleshire, 32, associate City Manager of Ontario, will be-come Puente's first City Man-ager when the newly incorpo-rated town begins function-ing Aug. 1.

Aleshire [...]

C. JAY MERCER, AIR FORCE VET, MOVES TO CITY STAFF

REDLANDS—C. Jay Mercer, the city's new assistant city manager and head of the accounting de-partment, has moved with his wife and two daughters to 433 Ash St.

Mercer, who graduated from a period of internship in the Coro Foundation, San Francisco, began duties with the city this week.

'Girl Friday For the U.N. Delegates

[F]RIDAY for the del[egates] of the sixty na[tions] [assemb]led at the [...] this week is f[...] [vol]unteer Mary Elle[n ...]

‸ger girl, guide, tel[ephone] [rece]ptionist, and maid[,] a sampling of t[...] [eas]ily taken on by t[...] [M]ary Ellen, the you[ng ...] ‸se "office" is rig[ht ...] [par]t of the delegate[s ...] she's an assista[nt ...]

A Trained Man For The Job

Bert DeLotto is a rare candidate. He has actually devoted a number of years to preparing himself for public office.

It is unfortunate that such a candidate is a rarity, but such is the case in American politics. We certainly hope that his efforts to train himself for public service will be re-warded by the voters of the First Supervisorial District.

DeLotto's studies and training have not been of an aca-demic nature.

He received a scholarship to study under the Coro Foun-dation grant, and spent a year in the San Francisco Bay Area studying county and municipal government. [His] studies might be likened to the on-the-job training giv[en ap]prentices.

Locally he took an active interest in considering [a] charter for the city of Fresno, and was one of the m[...] [...]tenders at the meetings of the study comm[ittee ...] [...]y the county charter. He has taken [...] [...]n politics, and has held many positi[ons ...] [...] his own party organizations (he ha[...]

[...] things have given DeLotto first han[d ...] [...]government functions, what the p[...] are, how to work with people politically and [...] things done.

Johnson named MP assistant city manager

City Manager C. L. Long of Menlo Park last night a[n]nounced the appointment [of] Administrative Assistant Jo[hn] R. Johnson to the newly created post of assistant cit[y] manager.

Johnson, a graduate of Stan-ford University and the Coro Foundation, public service in-stitution in San Francisco, h[as] been administrative assistant i[n] Menlo Park since September, 1952. He is married and has tw[o] small children.

THE INCREASING burden of municipal activitie[s ...]

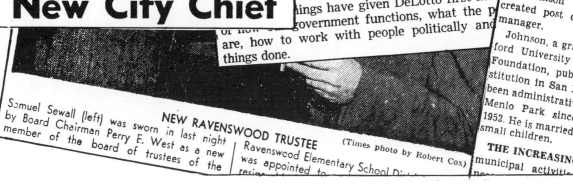

Samuel Sewall (left) was sworn in last night by Board Chairman Perry E. West as a new member of the board of trustees of the

NEW RAVENSWOOD TRUSTEE

(Times photo by Robert Cox)

Ravenswood Elementary School Di[strict. ...] was appointed to [...] resig[...]

laboratory course was held for business executives through Golden Gate College.

Throughout this period, the Internship was becoming recognized and established. Graduates achieved prominence as city managers, staff in the California legislature, elected officials, U.S. Treasurer, etc.

1968

Robert Coate, financial advisor and Coro grad/trustee, became president of Coro. WDF moved to Chairman of the Board after serving many years as chief fund raiser.

1969

Coro received a $100,000 grant from Ford to open an office in Pittsburgh. Bill Whiteside, former director of the LA office, was sent to open this office. However, because of economic recession, this venture did not succeed and the office was closed in 1970. This year Robert Coate resigned to go into politics, and Jack Steiny, a Coro trustee since 1947, became president.

1969

John Greenwood became Director/Trainer for Los Angeles, and David Sibbet was hired for a similar position in San Francisco in 1970. Don Fletcher transferred his major attention to the LA office.

1970

Senior staff John Robinson and Jerry Jones left the Foundation. Jack Steiny appointed David Sibbet Executive Director in San Francisco and John Greenwood Director in Los Angeles. The public trust form of organization for Coro was dissolved and Coro re-organized as a non-profit corporation. Tax exempt status in the most favorable category was granted by IRS. A large amount of debt (between $400,000 and $500,000) was forgiven by individuals to whom it was owed, and Coro reorganized free of debt except for $40,000 owed current vendors. This was a critical time for Coro. Continuation was only made possible by the heroic self sacrifice of individuals, including that of Robert Coate who personally guaranteed loans.

1971

Kathleen Schuler was hired to lead the S.F. Fellows program and Tom Layton, Richard Butrick, Susan Robinson and Melissa Bush joined the San Francisco staff.

William Whiteside, 1953*

John Robinson, 1951*

Jerry Jones, 1951*

* Coro application photographs

OBSERVATIONS ON CORO GRADUATES

By Robert L. Coate (1966 Coro Reports)

(Robert L. Coate is Vice President of Winfield & Co., San Francisco investment managers. A graduate of Stanford University, he was selected for Coro's 1948–49 Internship in Public Affairs. Since completing the internship, Bob has combined a business career with outstanding service in the public affairs field. Recently elected State Treasurer of the Democratic Party, he also was a successful candidate in 1961 for the Chabot College (Alameda County) Board of Trustees. In 1960 he became the first Coro alumnus to be appointed to Coro Foundations Board of Trustees. Bob travels extensively and has had the opportunity to become acquainted with many Coro graduates.)

Frequently I have been asked by Coro's president to call on a prospective sponsor or to address a group of prospective contributors to the support of the work of Coro. Long ago I learned not to analyze "What is Coro?" Discussing Coro's product—its graduates—answers the question far better than any mere description of its program.

Talking to Coro graduates has been an intriguing and practical time saver for me. I do business with Washington agencies and I have discovered how helpful it is to call the Coro office to find out whether a Coro graduate is working there. If so,

All IN GOOD FUN—Pete McClosky (Republican from the 11th CD) and Robert L. Coate, new Coro Foundation president, exchange good-natured jibes about each other's party affiliation at the last Fresno Alumni conference. Coate has given up partisan activities for Coro, but is still remembered for his state work in Democratic politics.

I call this stranger and in ten minutes I learn more than I might by going to Washington myself. With Coro graduates, I find it is easy to get to the point and to understand the circumstances involved. I have tried it many times with equal success in differing circumstances.

Coro people have an excellent sense of what America is all about. They realize that the complex interplay among government, business, labor and other institutions is in fact a system that already has gone far beyond the past century's titles, labels and slogans. People who get important tasks done are usually impressed with a foundation which helps younger people feel affirmative about our complicated system.

After many years of puzzling over the steps effective people use to get hard jobs done, I have come up with an oversimplified answer. Sense, consensus, consent. First, an idea must make sense to the proponent. Second, he usually talks it through with friends and associates for whose judgment he has regard, or perhaps with individuals whose views are likely to vary widely. The point is to seek consensus. Third, he seeks the consent of large numbers of people.

We who make up these large numbers of people are called "voters" by politicians, "markets" by businessmen, the "masses" by yearny thinkers, the "uncommitted" by hopefuls, etc. Whatever we are, not very much of real importance in America will take place unless a lot of us consent. Almost no one is smart enough to take an idea that makes sense to him and get our consent without having established prior consensus. On the other hand, we do not respond either well or long to one who espouses a consensus unless it seems clear to us that it makes sense to him also. Coro graduates seem to go through all three steps.

One other trait! Viet Nam and Mississippi nick at the Coro graduate. He is irked by people who rant at "politicians" but do nothing themselves. He assumes that the public sectors of our society are his personal responsibility. With the sense of common purpose, with accumulated experience and knowledge, any number of Coro graduates could be a worthwhile and impressive public force.

John Greenwood,
Executive Director, LA

1972

A grant was given by Danforth Foundation to open an office in St. Louis. Alex Hartley and Jim Schoning playing key roles in organizing training.

Executive Director was Don Kornblet, who spent a year in Los Angeles training to go to St. Louis. SF obtained a reorganization grant from the Oakes Trust of the San Francisco Foundation and developed the "Centers" model and changed the name "Interns" to "Fellows." Dick Butrick became Executive Director in San Francisco with Sibbet becoming Director of Training.

With the expansion of Coro to other sites, the need for a National Board of Governors was recognized. This Board was formed this year with the hope that a national identity could be achieved for Coro.

This year Mike Roos, the first non-Coro graduate to become a center director, was hired in LA. Mike later had a distinguished career in the California Legislature.

WDF resigned from the Coro Board to start up his separate training program, Liaison Citizens, going back to an original idea of working with citizens at every age and all levels in order to discover self-governing principles and to link agencies in the community. David Abel joined as Director of Training in LA.

Jack Steiny and David Sibbet confer about the San Francisco Center.

1975

Van Dyne Dodge died this year, leaving a large gap in the inspirational leadership of Coro.

1976–1979

Executive Directors in Los Angeles were: Jack Flanagan, Andrea Van de Kamp, Nancy York and Joanne Kozberg. During this period, Coro went from training twelve Fellows per year to several hundred in special programs such as: mid-career women's program (ARCO, Jewett Foundation); Junior League programs; Arts Managers (CBS grant); summer program for high school students; Business Managers Program and a program to assist new members of the California Assembly to their jobs in Sacramento.

The Annual Public Affairs Award Dinner grew from a small event to an LA institution which draws nearly 1,000 guests. The first national retreats for staff development were held as National Coro slowly formed. Coro Associates, was begun as a support organization.

An office was opened in Kansas City in 1976 and offered a summer Fellows program.

Dianne Wins

Dianne Feinstein, a Coro Graduate in 1956, made San Francisco history this last November by running first in a 15-way race for five seats on the San Francisco City and County Board of Supervisors.

Dianne is one of very few in the City's history to win against an incumbent for a seat and the first to head the list running as a non-incumbent.

Since her Coro Internship, Dianne established herself in San Francisco as an active worker in politics and community programs, as well as serving as an able appointee on several committees and boards dealing with the administration of criminal justice. She is wife of Dr. Bertram Feinstein, a neurosurgeon at Mount Zion Hospital and Medical Center in San Francisco.

1979–80

A New York Center was made possible by the assistance of other Coro Centers and the National Board of Governors. Jim Schoning played a prominent start-up role, and Mary Ellen Irwin continued her role as East Coast recruiter.

1981–86

Robin Kramer was director in Los Angeles. During the years she was there, Coro programming was diversified to include programs for Hispanic Law Students, Asian Leadership, Oxnard and Orange County programs.

Don Weddle of Opinion Research conducted the first survey of alumni in 1981. This survey established the value graduates placed upon their training and thus became important evaluation norm. The survey also showed the high rate of community activity which characterize Coro graduates.

1981–91

Martha Bredon was Executive Director in Northern Calif. The John Veneman Fund was initiated as the first scholarship fund for the Fellows Program. The Women's Program began. Agriculture Week was incorporated into the internships, recognizing the importance of agribusiness to California economy and ecology.

1982

Karen Eisele was hired as director in New York and served until 1993.

1984

The National Board of Governors appointed John McClosky to be the first National Coro Director. McClosky held a PhD in political science, was the St. Louis Executive Director and had held a position with the Danforth Foundation. However, this initiative was short-lived because of failure to work out the relationship with the Coro Centers. Marilyn Waite was hired subsequently as Director, but she, too, was not able to meld the whole organization together. The Board continued to function under a Chairperson, representatives from the Centers and some members at large.

The first Fellowship was offered this year in New York.

1986–89

Joan Anderson, then Peter Taylor served as Executive Directors in Southern California. Carol Tharp became Exec. Director in 1989 and continues to this writing.

1989

National Program Standards adopted by the National Board of Governors. Standards list vital elements which must be included in all Coro programs. Standard were reviewed by trainers from all the Centers. Fran Aleshire facilitated this process, wrote up and presented the standards to the National Board.

1990

The Centers became separately incorporated. "Foundation" was dropped from the name, and the official name became simply "Coro." Local centers form a confederation through articles of affiliation.

1990

The first "Summer Institute" for Coro staff was held at Ray Roeder's house in Aptos, California, for the purpose of providing continuing education for the professional staff.

1990

Neighborhood Leadership Programs began in Southern California to involve people at the grass roots in Coro progams and train for local leadership.

1995

Executive Directors at this writing are:
Coro Southern California, Carol Tharp.
Coro Northern California, Rozanne Junker
Coro Midwest, Sandra Lehrer
Coro Eastern, Maria Schneider
Coro Kansas City Office, Director/Training, Karen Stubbs

Training Directors are:
San Francisco, Lisa Lyons
Los Angeles, Ron Kurumoto
Midwest, Scott Staufer
Eastern, Melodye Serino

1976 SF/LA SEMINAR

Vic Fazio and Jim Schoning share Democratic and Republican perspectives on Sacramento for the combined San Francisco and Los Angeles interns. The briefing was just prior to the Intern's April Sacramento trip. Vic is currently consultant to the Majority Caucus in the Assembly. Jim is assistant to Bob Monagan, Minority Speaker in the Assembly. Both are graduates of the 1965 L.A. Internship. From left are Jim Schoning, Vic Fazio, Dick Butrick, Executive Director in San Francisco.

(This old Coro Reports photo was enhanced as much as possible—and included for its content value in spite of the moire patterns.)

In 1944 Bert Mattei, President of Honolulu Oil, suggested that Fletcher visit L.A. and "learn something of its political views and problems."

THE L.A., SOUTHERN CALIFORNIA STORY

Austin Woodward

SF '52–Training Staff LA, 1956

An early inter-office memo from Jerry Jones, then Director of Coro Northern California, to our little band of pioneers in Los Angeles—Bill Whiteside, Mary Farrell and myself—back in 1957 when we were gearing up for the first Southern California Internship in Public Affairs, expressed it nicely. Jerry's salutation was: "To our friends in Little America."

We felt that way. Starting out, the atmosphere seemed cold, remote and lonely compared to the warmth and acceptance which Coro had gained from San Francisco.

Los Angeles Exploration

Don Fletcher gave us the background leading to the start-up of the L.A. office in a one page memo. It said that in 1944 Bert Mattei, president of Honolulu Oil, suggested that Fletcher visit L.A. and "learn something of its political views and problems." In 1945, through introductions from George Cameron of the San Francisco Chronicle, WDF (these initials became Fletcher's shorthand signature) met Norman Chandler of the L.A. Times and Asa Call of Pacific Mutual.

In 1951 and 1952, George O'Brien of Standard Oil of California hosted two Coro luncheons "where Coro programs were presented to community business leaders." Fletcher observed that while no big contributions resulted, a few good friendships were formed that blossomed a few years later. During this early period contacts were also made with area colleges and universities, public officials, labor representatives and community leaders.

Fletcher's memo concluded: "In Coro's exploratory years, many approved of our goal of training able young people, but few stepped forward to assist."

The Big Five

A broad base of support was painfully slow to manifest. WDF had done fine spadework, but Coro was still a new and only vaguely understood organization when we opened the LA office in 1957.

I joined the staff in the Fall of 1956, moving to Northern California temporarily for training and orientation. Then, in March, 1957, my work began in LA when I moved back to Southern California and opened the L.A. office.

From the start, the big challenge was fund-raising. We had to establish a beachhead in the community's philanthropic budgets, essentially those of major corporate sponsors.

The first wedge came from North-South business relationships. From such ties, WDF enlisted what we came to call the "big four", a quartet of Southern California business leaders who introduced us around and became the nucleus of our Business Sponsorship Committee. They were: Philip Magruder, General Petroleum; Preston Hotchkis, Founders Insurance; Henry Mudd, Cyprus Mines; and Elvon Musick of the law firm Musick, Peeler & Garrett. Shortly afterwards, Fred Ortman, a former Gladding-McBean executive who was with the Stanford Research Institute, made it the Big Five.

Personally, I was somewhat shocked when I came to realize that none of these stalwart men, good and generous though they were, really had much depth of understanding or conviction about Coro.

They cheerfully committed themselves to promoting our cause with introductions and letters, but sometimes in unguarded moments they revealed only a foggy notion of the Coro mission. However, I remember fondly an occasion when I visited Henry Mudd during one of our periodic times of crisis. He wrote out a check on the spot with few questions asked.

The California Club Luncheon

One landmark event early in the game was a luncheon at the California Club to introduce Coro to influential leaders. In those days this club was the acknowledged hub and headquarters of the corporate power structure. Having an event there was the traditional step to credibility in L.A.

Invitations went out from the Big Five to key business leaders for a luncheon on March 6, 1957. Guests included Fred Fagg, president of USC, and Arthur Coons, president of Occidental. Van Dyne Dodge came down from San Francisco and at least two program alumni, Frank Aleshire and Garth Lipsky, were present. Mr. Dodge was superb. "Business cannot afford NOT to support efforts like this," he said. WDF was his usual spellbinding self; the alumni spoke compellingly of the effect on their careers, and a lively question and answer period followed. The event was judged a big success.

Coro had landed in the Southern California pond, and ripples began to spread.

Show and Tell

The doors of the Coro Southern California office opened officially April 1, 1957. Our first home was in the Commercial Exchange Building at 416 W. 8th Street, a little on the fringe of downtown but still convenient to city and county offices and corporate headquarters. Later we moved to 1220 Wilshire, a wonderful old house with some blessed parking spaces.

Our offices were strongly reminiscent of the S.F. office space. I was able to purchase a set of fine, sturdy banker's chairs at bargain prices from my old employer, Union Oil, when they moved into their new headquarters. I believe some of these chairs are still in use, decades later, and, again, they were much like the chairs remembered by interns who twisted and turned in them as they tried to answer WDF's questions in San Francisco.

I was soon joined by seasoned SF staffers, Bill Whiteside and Mary Farrell (soon to become Mary Kehew). They quickly established Coro's competence as they laid the groundwork for internship assignments in government, labor, political and community realms. They also worked in academia, recruiting and setting up the laboratory course.

We continued our outreach. Aside from "show and tell" presentations, we began the tradition of a Southern California Selection Day. We invited influential local leaders to be on the selection panel and participate in a day crammed with challenging exercises. Another time, the San Francisco Interns came to L.A. and put on a "show-and-tell" for another California luncheon. Now we could introduce real, live, earnest Coro interns who were in training and most impressive with their enthusiasm and idealism.

Our local alumni were indispensable. They briefed us as to what was going on in the Southland and opened doors with introductions. Prime among these people were city managers Craig McMicken, Frank Aleshire, Jay Mercer, George Aiassa, Glenn Kendall and Bob Vollmer. Dick and Tina Lower, '54 and '52 internship graduates, Lani Weirick ('54) and Ruth James, an honorary alumna who had been on the SF staff for years, acted as adjunct staff members on occasions, as did my '52 classmate and life partner, Rosalie Stuart Woodward. We have the distinction of being the first "Coro couple."

Other alumni prominent in our early L.A. efforts included Sam Sewall, Hank Rose, Dick Manning, Jack Miller, Bud Aronson, Garth Lipsky, Bob Christopherson, Tom Dooley, Ollie Peter and Marty Ostrow. Our graduates made it all possible and enjoyable.

Breaking into the Budgets

We were disappointed in not being able to field a class in 1957–58, but the money wasn't there. Early contributors got our hopes up, though. Carnation Company, Broadway Department Stores, Union Oil, Richfield, Southern California Edison and Southern Counties Gas are ones that stand out in my memory.

We just had not anticipated the difficulty of breaking into contribution budgets for the first time. Over and over we were told, "We're fully committed." They were used to giving to such established organizations as Boy Scouts, Junior Achievement, and the World Affairs Council. "But we appreciate what you are doing," one said, and then he presented me with an engraved ashtray and lighter.

The successes we achieved were usually through individuals who had "been there" in the political-public affairs realm. The public affairs man at Richfield Oil, for example, was Rodney Rood, who had once been an assistant in the L.A. mayor's office. He was a big help to Coro. At Southern California Edison there were layers of people from governmental affairs man Ron Ketcham to their chairman, William Mullendore. These people had long honed their skills in contacts with local, country, state and federal government. They understood and appreciated Coro's approach.

Others remained suspicious. This was, after all, the era of Senator McCarthy and the John Birch Society. Mary Farrell had an introduction from Pierre Salinger, then of the SF Chronicle to Captain Hamilton, head of the L.A. Police Department's secret Intelligence Division, and this connection enabled us to assure jittery inquirers that Coro was "O.K." We had a harder time with a private "intelligence service" with some corporate subscribers. They were suspicious about our government and labor contacts.

Support Arrives from Many Sources

Organized labor was very receptive to Coro Foundation. With warm endorsements from the S.F. area, Bill Whiteside developed substantial support, including contributions, from a broad base of labor organizations. Members of our Southern California Advisory Committee included top officials such as Thomas Pitts, president of the California State Federation of Labor; Bill Bassett of the L.A. County Central Labor Council; Sig Arywitz of the T.L.G Workers Union; Ed Shedlock of the Utility Workers; Al Lunceford of the Greater L.A. CIO Council and George O'Brien of the Electrical Workers.

Mary Farrell, in the meantime, was busy working in the corridors of city hall and the county administration building. She gathered pledges of support for our "soon to come" Coro class of interns. There were some outstanding figures on the local governmental scene in these days. I remember County Administrative Officer Arthur Will; City Administrative Officer Samuel Leask, Jr. (our first graduation speaker; L.A. City Council President John Gibson, and Georgianna Hardy of the L.A. City School Board, and there were many, many more who went out of their way to provide cooperation and support.

These were eventful times, too. Mary went to observe one history-making city council session and was greeted by a sign specifying, "FOR the Dodger contract, sit on left—AGAINST the Dodger contract, sit on right." Ever mindful of Coro's non-partisan status, Mary remained standing, frozen, in the doorway, engulfed by TV cameras, lights and the press.

A Jump Start from Ford

Coro was warmly greeted by local colleges and universities who began guiding many of their most promising graduates to apply for Coro scholarships. Schools like USC who had their own internship programs were wary at first, but T.J. Anderson in the Political Science Department and Carolyn Heine from the USC Law School soon became enthusiastic supporters.

Ivan Hinderaker, Dean McHenry and Winston Crouch were interested allies at UCLA; Raymond McKelvey of Occidental, and John Vieg of Pomona were others who became devoted partisans. We needed this academic seal of approval for recruitment and selection but also to support our applications to foundation and corporate funders.

At last, it was a foundation that saved the day. Sifting through a few old files to help write this reminiscence, I found a yellowed clipping that tells the essentials.

Dated May 19, 1958, it announced a $258,000 Ford Foundation "matching fund" grant for Coro Foundation, mainly to assist Coro's Internship in Public Affairs programs in San Francisco and Los Angeles. While that grant didn't solve all our financial problems, it was the booster which fueled our launch in Southern California. The class of 1958–59 was soon selected and on its way to history as L.A.'s first.

I've always thought of the Ford Foundation grant as just another rabbit that W. Donald Fletcher pulled from his hat. He had a way of doing that.

I've always thought of The Ford Foundation grant as just another rabbit that W. Donald Fletcher pulled from his hat. He had a way of doing that.

Austin woodward

CORO GETS FORD GRANT

BI-PARTISAN BACKERS — Republican Lt. Governor Robert Finch (left) and Democratic Assembly Speaker Jesse Unruh examine the roster of current Coro Foundation Interns with W. Donald Fletcher, Coro President and Co-Founder. Finch and Unruh are honorary statewide co-chairmen of a $200,000 fundraising drive aimed at broadening Coro's sources of support.

CORO EXPANSION TO THE MIDWEST

by Don Kornblut and Robert Ellerman, Jr.

While Coro's first St. Louis internship program was established in Septmber, 1973, the seeds for starting up Coro's Midwestern Center were actually planted a decade earlier. Coro's co-founder, Don Fletcher, had been visiting officials of the Danforth Foundation, explaining Coro's mission and methodology. By 1970, the Danforth Foundation and its Vice-President and later president, Gene Schwilk, became convinced that Coro could make a difference in the St. Louis community. It was this relationship that paved the road for the Coro Midwestern Center.

St. Louis leader and early Coro supporter Thomas Latzer had this to say about the impression Don Fletcher made upon him: "*Don Fletcher is incisive and vigorous, a gentleman and a delight to be around. He is able to understand young people and to stimulate their thought processes. He can draw out of them answers they had not previously realized they had. He is a true and skillful educator.*"

Both Don Fletcher and the Danforth Foundation believed that Coro's rigorous training program would inspire talented young men and women to develop an understanding of public affairs and a commitment to the St. Louis community. St. Louis had a history of racial polarization, and it was their hope that Coro graduates, particularly minority graduates, could benefit from their training and contribute toward healing some of the divisions within the community.

Danforth Foundation Makes it Possible

The first selection Coro held in St. Louis took place in 1970 at Washington University. Two individuals, Mike Geiger and Paul Mandalback, were selected and sent through the California programs that year. At the same time, the Danforth Foundation announced a six year, $600,000 grant for establishing a Coro Midwestern Center in St. Louis. There was immediate interest in St. Louis about who and what Coro was, its background, and what it intended to do in St. Louis. To allow sufficient time for planning and development, a two-year period (1971–73) was designated to introduce Coro into the community properly.

Coro named Don Kornblet as the first Executive Director. A graduate of the Coro Los Angeles internship (1967), Don was a native St. Louisan who had returned to St. Louis and had begun a public affairs career with the Urban League of St. Louis. Don's early Coro responsibilities included spending time in the Coro Los Angeles office so that he could learn the management of the organization while he also continued to work on laying the groundwork for the work he was to do in St. Louis.

Los Angeles board trustee Jack Steiny was a strong influence in Coro's early administration of the Danforth Foundation grant. Jack brought his business acumen and much needed skills to help stabilize the organization, following a period of rapid change and lean income.

Three main initiatives were agreed upon during the 1971–73 period: 1) recruitment and development of a strong Board; 2) efforts to win the support of community and corporate individuals and groups; and 3) recruitment, orientation and training of staff.

Board development proceeded swiftly. George S. Rosborough, Jr., a prominent St. Louis business and community leader, took an interest in Coro and became the first chairman. Much of Coro's success can be attributed to his leadership. Other founding board members included: Dr. Leigh Gerdine, president of Webster University; Mrs. Emily Ullman, community leader; N. Howard Nilson, general manager of Western Electric Company, and Mrs. Weldon "Sugar" Smith, another prominent community leader.

A series of luncheon meetings were arranged by Mr. Rosborough, and these meetings provided the vehicle for gaining important community support. One was hosted by Clarence C. Barksdale, Chairman and CEO of First National Bank in St. Louis and Donald E. Lasater, Chairman and CEO of Mercantile Bank. This meeting set up important contacts. Momentum gathered, and soon financial and program support came from such firms as Monsanto, Union Electric Company, Pet, Inc., Ralston Purina, Emerson Electric Co., Laclede Gas Company, and Southwestern Bell Telephone. Eventually other leading firms, including Anheuser-Busch Companies, Inc., General Dynamics, Mallinckrodt Chemical Company, and May Company Department Stores became Coro supporters. Many of these firms become long term and continuing donors and supporters.

Civic Progress Supports

These firms were members of a St. Louis network called Civic Progress, and their acceptance of Coro provided an early barometer for Coro's acceptance by the St. Louis business establishment. By 1991, an early Coro St. Louis graduate, Al Kerth, had become Executive Secretary of Civic Progress.

Another prominent early supporter and significant patron of Coro's was Thomas Latzer, Vice-President of Pet, Inc. and a member of the founding family of that company. Of Coro Latzer stated: "*When I first heard of Coro, I was particularly impressed with the way it builds on diversity. Coro offers diversity of participants, of programs and of experience. Too often citizenship or leadership training programs tend to expose participants to a one-sided view of life. For example, a business sponsored fellowship tends to present business in a most favorable light while labor unions sponsor programs with a bias toward their interests. Coro gives its participants views from all angles, thus giving them an opportunity to form more educated opinions. I feel, more strongly than ever, that society benefits from having leaders who know where other people are coming from. If we can have even a few leaders who understand each other and who are devoted to improving the community as a whole, we will all benefit.*"

Both Don Fletcher and the Danforth foundation believed that Coro's rigorous training program would inspire talented young men and women to develop an understanding of public affairs and a commitment to the St. Louis community.

DONALD R. KORNBLET, new Midwest Director of the Coro Foundation in St. Louis (right) discusses the upcoming establishment of an Internship program with William E. Douthit, Executive Director of the Urban League of St. Louis. Kornblet served as the Director of Public Education for the League since 1968.

In order to develop further community contacts and introduce Coro to a broader segment of the region, Coro held annual Selection meetings in St. Louis in 1971 and 1972. These sessions, plus several individual meetings with key community leaders, helped build a base for better understanding, future training assignments, referrals of candidates for the Fellows Program and financial support. Through all of these activities, much good will and enthusiasm already existed for the program when the first internship was launched in 1973.

First Staff

Coro's first staff included, besides Don Kornblet, Alex Hartley as director of training and Maria Wagstaff, a Coro graduate of the San Francisco program, as program and recruiting consultant. Alex was recruited from the Los Angeles Coro center where he had gone through the Coro Fellows program in 1971, along with Don West, a St. Louisan who succeeded Alex as trainer in 1975.

Significant interaction occurred among all the Coro centers at this time. Regular visits among staff and board members from San Francisco, Los Angeles and St. Louis brought the benefits of experience and wisdom to all. A sense of excitement pervaded the whole organization at this first expansion of Coro beyond California. An earlier attempt to move to Pittsburgh had fallen short of adequate funding, and Danforth was anxious not to let this happen in St. Louis.

All of the elements here described converged to make the Coro beginnings in St. Louis a big success. From its first office at 4378 Lindell, in an old mansion converted into office space, Coro started its Midwest journey. By this date in 1995, Coro graduates can be identified as playing significant leadership roles in St. Louis. Additionally, because of its impact in the Midwest, in 1975 Coro received an initial grant of $25,000 from the Kansas City Association of Trusts and Foundations and was thereby able to start a summer internship program in Kansas City. This program has continued successfully for the twenty years since that time and has earned a very favorable reputation for Coro.

Possibly the greatest impact has been on participants. One graduate of the Fellows Program says: " *Coro tries to expose its participants to as many facets of society as possible. Coro's ability to gather a diverse group of participants and then expose them to the widest possible range of experiences made a lasting impression on me. I sometimes refer to this process as 'knocking the corners off square pegs.' Because of Coro I have a completely different way of approaching experience."*

Yes! Coro has become a presence in St. Louis and the Midwest and continues as an innovative and enthusiastic member of the Coro family.

Founders Strategies Work!

From reading the accounts of Coro's growth into new areas, one can generalize that the pioneering work of the founders played a large role. Fletcher and Dodge understood the dynamics of communities. They knew the importance of tapping into the the network of those who make decisions, and from this knowledge, they learned how to reach out and cultivate those who knew how things worked and how to move projects forward. They also understood that relationships were crucial. Heavy handed intrusion was never their style; instead, they approached each community with respect for its logic and for its leaders. In this way, Coro was adopted by four quite different communities and very quickly became a major contributor to building the strength and integrity of each community.

Yes! Coro has become a presence in St. Louis and the Midwest.

CORO KANSAS CITY

by Karen Stubbs

Coro came to Kansas City in 1976, as an adjunct office of the Midwestern Center in St. Louis. Roe Taliaferro's recollection is that a number of Kansas City leaders were looking for ways to help business participate in the democratic process. Coro was a natural! There was a meeting at the Kansas City Life Insurance Company hosted by Marshall Chatfield. Don Kornblet, St. Louis Executive Director, met with civic leaders, including Bill Hall, Charles Kimball, H. Roe Taliaferro, George Lehr, James Kemper, Louise Levitt, and Dorothy Shea. Dorothy remembers attending a presentation of the St. Louis Fellows' class and being so impressed with the concept of Coro that she told Don Kornblet that "if there were ever any interest in a summer program in Kansas City that she would like to be a part of it." So . . .

First Class

Coro selected its first class for the summer of 1976 Dorothy Shea was the on-site coordinator and arranged for the placements. The format was a ten-week "mini Fellows" program, with rotations through the sectors, and interviews, seminars and simulations. Dale Flowers, Los Angeles Coro Fellow, was the trainer for that inaugural class. The following year, 1977, Jim Levitt (who had been in the 1976 class) and Don West, Fellows Trainer from St. Louis, were in charge of the program. Sharon Craig was Program Director in 1978 and 1979. Then . . .

In 1980, the National Board of Governors moved to elevate Coro Kansas City to a position of an Independent Office. That gave the local Board of Directors complete control over all aspects of the program. Original Kansas City Board members included Marjorie Allen, Joanne Collins, Alan Farris ('76), Mark Fountain, Bill Hall, Charles Kimball, Louise Levitt, Archie McGee, Marcia McGilley ('79), Tim McNamara ('77), I.J. Mnookin, Dan Slickman, Dottie Stafford, Beverly Norman Weishar, Floyd Wood and John Uhlmann. Roe Taliaferro was Board Chairman.

Coro Kansas City went through a rite of passage in 1985. Alter a process of self-evaluation, a group of board members took the responsibility to revitalize Coro. At the time the bank account totaled $4.51. A reconsti-

tuted board took the lead in raising the money to keep Coro alive. The dedication of the co-executive directors, Paula Thomson and Kyle Robinson, and the leadership of John McClosky, President of national Coro, was essential to the success of the reorganization. Karen Stubbs became the new Chairman, Roe Taliaferro came back from retirement to be vice-chair. Jan Stacy ('76) was a stalwart in those transitional days. Others who believed that Coro was important to Kansas City and were willing to serve on the new board included Bert Bates, Ruth Blake, Michael Braude, Mark Bredemeier ('79), Gene Eubanks, Tracy Burdette ('78), Mark Larrabee, Mike Loeb, Lisa Leonard, David Lillard, Cathy Rocha, Dorothy Shea, Gene Shipman, Harry Spring, Bill Sproull ('81), Linda Thornton, and Kent Whittaker.

Voluteer Leaderships

Coro Kansas City has been fortunate to have good volunteer leadership. Board Chairs have included Roe Taliaferro ('80–'81), Archie McGee ('81–'82), Bruce Morgan ('82–'83), Susan Linden McGreevy ('83–'84), Karen Stubbs ('84–'86), Kent Whittaker ('86–'87), Ken Weiner, Coro '80, ('88–'89), Perry Brandt ('89–'90), Duanna Linville Dralus ('90–'91), Phil Hanson, Coro '81, ('91–'92), John Stormer, Coro '83, ('92–'94), Karen Glickstein, Coro '84, ('94–'95) and Vernon Voorhees ('95–'96).

Dee Lyons was appointed the first real Kansas City Executive Director in December, 1980. Dee served as Executive Director through the 1982 class year, and was succeeded by Kay Waldo Barnes, who was on the City Council of Kansas City. Kay served for one year ('83), and in 1984 was replaced by Paula Thomson and Kyle Robinson. Paula and Kyle shared the job for three years, and in 1987 Pat Wright became Executive Director. Pat trained the classes of 1987, 1988, and 1989. Vicki Barham replaced her in 1990, and served for five years, until Karen Stubbs succeeded her in 1995. Throughout the years, there have been periodic visits from Coro trainers loaned from other centers to help with the "Coro Tools" part of the program. Don West, Alex Hartley, Robbyn Stewart, Scott Stauffer, and Ron Kuramoto all have worked with the Kansas City interns. There are records from 1978, in plaintive letters from St. Louis, that the job of heading Kansas City Coro was more than one person could reasonably do. In 1995 we still run a one-person office, with the Executive Director also acting as Trainer, Development Director, and Secretary. If the computer hadn't been invented, we would be out of business.

While we don't have a United States Senator yet, we do have illustrious alumni—lawyers, journalists, professors, doctors, not-for-profit executives, moms, and entrepreneurs. There were Coro alumni serving at the same time as Jackson County Chairmen of both the Democratic, Tim McNamara ('77) and Republican, Mark Bredemeier ('79) parties.

Coro Kansas City just graduated its twentieth class. There were seven graduates and five college seniors representing eight colleges in the group. The composition was a typical Coro class—diverse in every way you could imagine. Our Selection Day is modeled after the Fellows, our Interns follow the natural progression of Coro—Logic Study, First Presentation, Blitz Week, Not-For Profit Week, Government Week, Business Week, Labor Week (complete with a mock negotiation with the Federal Mediators), Media Week assignments and Seminars. The interns spend a day learning leadership styles in a challenge course, have mock trials in front of federal judges, and interview the movers and shakers in the metro area. Kansas City is bisected by the Missouri/Kansas state line, so there are lots of opportunites to intersect with governments. We end the ten-week program with a group project and graduation.

The Kansas City model is one which would work anywhere. Fund raising is never easy, but the appeal of a college program is that it is cheaper than the Fellows program, and it is partially sold on the hope that it will keep young leaders in the community. Kansas City is proud to have had pioneered the "short program" concept. We are fortunate to have had civic leaders with the foresight to bring Coro to Kansas City in 1976.

Kansas City is Proud to have pioneered the "short program concept". . . . it's a model which would work anywhere.

HOW CORO CAME TO THE NEW YORK, EASTERN CENTER

by Kenneth Mountcastle, Karin Eisele and
early board members

The First Glimmers

Coro appeared on the East Coast in the late 1960's. Initially the effort was to recruit candidates for the Fellows Program. Mary Ellen Irwin, a Coro Fellows graduate, was the first recruiter, and she was succeeded by Grace Alexander. Successful candidates were routed to Coro programs In Los Angeles, San Francisco or St. Louis.

During the early 1970's, Richard Butrick, Executive Director in San Francisco, began making annual trips to the East Coast to develop contacts and consider the possibilities of Coro's expansion to the East. Since Coro had an office in Pittsburgh for eighteen months during this period, there was ample reason for these exploratory trips. Butrick established a relationship with Pitney Bowes at IBM, and this led to meeting Benjamin Van Wormer who was Vice-President for Public Affairs at American-Standard. Van Wormer began to form a small board in New York City to cover the expenses of Selection Day. He enlisted his counterparts in several major companies and succeeded in attracting Edward Weidein from Union Carbide, George Finnegan from McGraw-Hill, Margaret Longley, New York Times and Helen Brown, CBS. Other trustees during these early stages were Alice Baker, Barbara Williamson, and Lowell Dodge. This networking effort, linked with using Coro graduates, illustrates the strategy whereby Coro was able to move into new areas.

During the late 1970's, Van Wormer was recruited onto the National Board of Governors. At a Board meeting in St. Louis, summer of 1978, Don Livingston made a motion to open a New York office. The motion passed even though New York had no program, a small board and little money. The local board agreed to raise $60,000 to open the Center, and Truda Jewett was hired to take over recruiting duties. Truda started operations out of her home.

The Center Opens

Truda Jewett became Executive Director when the Center opened in the Fall of 1980. An office was located on the 9th Floor at 20 W. 40th Sreet in the Willkie Memorial Building of Freedom House. Van Wormer found this office when he noted a sign in the window on his way to his own office. He inquired and found one office located in a walk-up on the 9th floor since the elevator stopped at the 8th floor, The space was rented for $9 per square foot or $1,000 per month.

Several new board members were added at this time: Hamilton Kean, whose brother became Governor of New Jersey; Edward Lamont, retired banker from Morgan Guaranty Trust Company, and Donald Baker, Director of Community Relations for American Standard. The goal of the Center this year was to start up a program for women in 1981 since women's issues were top priority on the national agenda at that point.

The women's program, which was designed to last ten weeks, began with a two and a half day Logic Study and finished with a week in Albany, N.Y. to observe the legislature. The program was named Public Affairs for Mid-Career Women and was selected over the Fellows Program because less money was required and training capability at that time was very limited. But the program was very successful under the able leadership of Pat Koch Thaler, a sister of Mayor Ed Koch. She became the first Training Director. Pat spent the summer in Los Angeles as a participant in their women's program. Another influx of Coro experience came when Joyce Ream, who had run the women's program in San Francisco moved to New York to assist Thaler as consultant in the Spring of 1981. Grace Hughes, a former director of the women's program in San Francisco, also came to New York to assist Thaler at that time. The first Selection Day was held on February 27, 1981 with Mayor Ed Koch as guest speaker, and the program began the next month with twelve participants.

Four of the programs for Mid-Career Women were conducted as well as a program in the Fall of 1982 for the Commission on the Status of Women. Jewell Jackson McCabe, who was Director of Community Affairs at WNET, Channel 13, was instrumental in involving Coro in this program along with Dr. Marcella Maxwell, Academic Dean at Medger Evans College. Gradually staff members were added: Claudia Grose, Assistant to the Program Director; Heidi Briegar to do recruiting, and Laura Lijewski, a graduate of the Women's Program in Los Angeles volunteered to work in the office and produce a newsletter.

Consolidation of the Program

At a December 17, 1980 Board meeting there was good news. Coro had raised $121,800, half of the money needed for the coming year. Strong new board members joined up: Jewell Bickford, Coro graduate Tim Hollister, Kenneth Mountcastle, Debbie Scott, Kathleen Brown, Ruth Santiago, and Judith Berek, V.P. for the National Union of Hospital and Health Care Employees.

Trude Jewett resigned as Executive Director in August, 1982, so the Board had to fill the void. Program commitments were fulfilled by Claudia Grose and Meryl Greenfield, a graduate of the program. Sharon Butler was loaned from the Los Angeles Center to provide support and to help with recruitment of a new Director. The Center became almost dormant during most of 1983. Ken Mountcastle had succeeded Van Wormer as Board Chairman, and he tells of the tough times at that juncture. Fortunately, the issue was resolved with the hiring of Karin Eisele who ushered in a period of stable leadership. In the meantime, Kathleen Brown had become more involved with the Coro Board, and she was instrumental in bringing Meredith Brokaw into the fold.

When Karin joined the staff, she had a skeleton training staff and very few resources. Her first task was to reactivate the development program and add new programs. During the leadership gap, funding cycles of major supporters were missed, so new proposals had to be generated, and quickly. Meryl Greenfield was full of new ideas for specific constituencies. There was a need for leadership among neighborhood and ethnic groups. Philip Morris was a supporter of many programs for people of Hispanic origin, so a program was designed to meet this need. Philip Morris funded four consecutive programs for Hispanic Women. Other special, fee for service programs were designed. Coro ran summer programs for minority high school students in Newark, in conjunction with the Newark Collaborative.

The Center began to make plans to start up a Fellows Program, but cash flow was still a serious problem. The other three Centers joined together and loaned the Eastern Center $50,000 to bridge the gap.

Fellows Program and Successful Fund Raising

Planning for the Fellows Program became a top priority, and an expression of intent was made to the National Board of Governors. The Board set $400,000 as the budget needed to start-up the Fellows Program. Devel-opment efforts accelerated. In the Spring of 1984, Eisele and Mountcastle called the National Board and identified the funding sources which would produce the needed money. The go-ahead signal was given, and the first Coro Fellows progam began in September, 1984. To augment the local training staff, Jim Schoning was transferred from Los Angeles to head up the training of Fellows.

Obviously, some major fund raising event was needed. Kathleen Brown and Meredith Brokaw assumed responsibility for a Spring event which would feature the first class of Fellows. They approached the CEO's of RCA, CBS and American Express to underwrite the event which was to be a gala dinner. The program was to honor Peter Ueberroth, Time Magazine Man of the Year. Three Coro Fellows were to interview him with Tom Brokaw acting as Moderator. Governor Mario Cuomo was a guest speaker. He was to welcome Coro to New York.

What a great evening! Guests were enthusiastic, and the evening produced a net profit of $80,000. This event was the first of Coro's Leadership Dinners, which have continued to be successful. The dinner enabled the Center to pay off its debts to the other Centers. The format of using three Coro Fellows continued, and Art Buchwald served as Moderator for the second dinner. Gradually the program changed so that other people currently in the news could be featured. One year the program honored Ross Perot and Felix Rohatyn. Later honorees were Tom Wolfe and Spike Lee. After the 1988 election, we had Lee Atwater and Ron Brown; after the 1992 election, Mary Matalin and James Carville. Other media stars have included Peter Jennings, Tim Russert, Cokie Roberts, Gwen Ifil, Michell McQueen, Roger Rosenblatt and Charlie Rose. The dinners were increasingly prominent and produced revenues of $200,000. The Center built up reserve of $300,000.

Relocation and Program Development

We were given notice to vacate our property in February, 1985 when the building was sold. At first no compensation was to be given for relocation expenses, but outraged tenants hired an attorney who had connections to the Office of the Secretary of State in Albany. A settlement was negotiated. Coro was paid $75,000 which paid for a move into a larger space at 95 Madison Avenue near 29th Street.

Coro was making good progress with a broad range of programs and a budget which had grown to $1,000,000. Meredith Brokaw became Chairman of the Eastern Center in 1985, and Ken Mountcastle moved to become Chairman of the National Board of Governors.

By this time, Steve Redfield, a Fellows graduate, had joined the training staff to assist Jim Schoning. Coro ran programs in the Bronx and conducted programs with the Junior League in Washington, D.C. The Eastern Center became more involved with the nation's capitol when the Henry M. Jackson Foundation gave the Center funding for a six week summer program for Fellows graduates from any Center. A Washington Council was formed to try and secure permanent funding from Washington sources.

During this period, new members of the Board were Walter Gips, Judy Dawkins, Jewell Jackson McCabe, Linda Gosden Robinson, Anne Addington, Millie Harmon-Myers, Ginny Ueberroth, Valery Newman, Fred Terrell, John Rose, Lolis Steckler, Mike Grobstein and Jane Hartley. Chairperson, Meredith Brokaw, deserves great credit for the growth and prosperity of the Eastern Center. The budget had grown in excess of one million dollars, the staff numbered 12, and a critical mass of alumni was developing.

New Programs

A new partnership was begun about this time when Meredith Brokaw and Jewell McCabe, who were on the Board of the New York Partnership, started up the Coro Leadership New York Program. The New York City Partnership members are major corporations and foundations; they provide funding for the Partnership's programs. Linking this great resource with Coro was a major break-through.

Leadership New York, now co-sponsored by Coro and the New York City Partnership, was established to nurture the leadership which will guide New York City into the next century. Participants are mid-career executives from the public, private and not-for-profit sectors with proven records of civic accomplishments. Each year thirty-five participants meet one full day and one evening a month, October through June. This program takes participants behind the scenes to learn first hand about city issues. Through a Coro-type format, participants grapple with complex urban issues and seek new ways to improve life in the City. They hear diverse views

New York has shown how Coro can partner with leadership programs, bringing the benefit of Coro's proven training methodology to make the programs more effective.

from policy makers, service providers, academics, community activists and community officials. Group discussions and training by Coro's skilled staff help them to make sense of their experiences and gain a sense of how their knowledge can be used to benefit New York.

Leadership New York is one of more than seven hundred programs nation-wide that are training civic leaders. New York has shown how Coro can partner with one of these programs, bringing the benefit of Coro's proven training approach and methodology to make the program more effective.

New Challenges and Transitions

In 1992, Karin Eisele left Coro, and a search committee was formed to find a successor. Karin had done an outstanding job for ten years and provided the stability and energy needed to get the program established. Problems were developing at Coro, and expenses began to eat into reserves. David Condliffe, a lawyer with wide experience, was chosen as the new Executive Director and joined Coro in October, 1992. David had been on the staff of Mayor David Dinkins prior to joining Coro. But the economic climate was deteriorating, and raising funds became increasingly difficult. Through all the lean times, the Fellows Program has been put on -at this writing, for ten years. Leadership New York also continues and adds to Coro's prestige in the community. Through the assistance of Board member, Ida Schmertz, Coro was able to move into new space in downtown Manhattan at 1 Whitehall Street.

David Condliffe left the staff in April, 1994 for another position, and another search committee went to work. Impressive candidates applied for the position of Executive Director. Fortunately Coro was able to obtain the services of Maria Schneider who had been Condliffe's administrative assistant at City Hall. At first her tenure was to be temporary, but in October 1994, she was named to the position permanently. In that same month, Fred Terrell, a Coro graduate from Los Angeles, succeeded Jewell Jackson McCabe as Board Chairperson.

During the fifteen year existence of the Coro Eastern Center, approximately 1000 persons have completed Coro programs. The Coro Fellows Program has graduated 120; Leadership New York 200, and the rest have participated in many special programs. The challenge for the Eastern Center, as for others, is to keep the Board and staff equal to the quality of the programs and participants. Coro has a fine reputation in New York and a remarkable record of achievement. The demands for Coro training continue to grow, and these demands represent a tremendous opportunity for the Eastern Center to make a contribution to leadership in New York and the nation's capitol.

THE START UP OF THE CORO NATIONAL ALUMNI ASSOCIATION

It was the summer of 1988 when a small group of people gathered in the Los Angeles offices of Coro to explore how alumni could show stronger support for Coro and for each other. The people who gathered on that day were Ray Roeder (SF Fellow, 63); Fran and Frank Aleshire (SF Fellow 48); Martha Bredon, then Executive Director of the Northern California Center; Lani Weirick, SF Fellow 54); Peter Taylor, then Executive Director of Southern California and a 1981 LA Fellow. This meeting marked the beginning of the CNAA, Coro National Alumni Association.

Starting with a Reunion

The first inspired idea of this group was to invite all Coro graduates up to 1972 to a weekend gathering, a reunion, to see what an expanded group might think about a continuing organization. The site selected was Asilomar Conference Center in Pacific Grove near Monterey. An early March weekend was picked for a date, and on that Friday night, a hundred people, graduates, staff and spouses, gathered at a reception to renew old friendships and begin a lively two days of discussion and planning. Quickly it became obvious how strong the bonds were in the group, even though we had not seen each other in many years. As one speaker summed it up, "The Coro orientation makes you feel just a bit like an alien in the the world after Coro, but here, we are at home." By the time of parting Sunday, a Steering Committee was formed, and a July 1989 meeting was planned for Oxnard, California.

The Oxnard meeting resulted in the decision to have another Asilomar conference that Fall. This time Coro's founder, W. D. Fletcher, took part in the program. Some key decisions were made to include graduates of special programs, spouses, staff and interested friends in the association. Also, a strong desire was expressed to be more than a California organization, but rather, to encourage a nationally-based Coro. We could say that November, 1989, Asilomar, marked the members' decision to go forward with the CNAA.

Quickly it became obvious how strong the bonds were in the group, even though we had not seen each other in many years.

By-laws, prepared by Jack Fine, were adopted and officers and directors were elected at a January meeting of the Coro National Board of Governors in 1909. The CNAA was designated the official alumni association of Coro. Later that year, CNAA received a 501 (C)3 designation as a separate non-profit entity.

Mission of the CNAA

The purposes of the organization were to: 1) promote the best interests of Coro, its staff, program participants and graduates, wherever located; 2) foster communications and a spirit of friendship, assistance and cooperation among all the graduates of Coro's various programs; 3) encourage and promote beneficial relations with and support of Coro by its alumni; and 4) contribute to the betterment of our communities, states and nation, through on-going Coro and Coro-alumni programs, including continuing education for graduates and others.

Accomplishments in the First Five Years of CNAA

Periodic publication of The Corospondent, a newsletter containing information about the activities of CNAA, Coro alumns and Coro Centers.

Publication of the Alumni Directory in 1992 containing available information on Coro graduates and mailed to all graduates of record.

A first Conference for all graduates was held in Phoenix, Arizona in November 1990 with three days of outstanding program, entertainment, and socializing. Video and graphics preserved memories of the first fifty years.

A second Conference was held in St. Louis in October, 1991, celebrating the opening of new Midwestern Center offices.

The celebration of the 50th Anniversary of the founding of Coro in San Francisco in 1942 by Donald W. Fletcher and Van Dyne Dodge was celebrated during three exciting days and our third Conference in Washington D.C., April, 1992.

1993 Annual Alumni Conference at Asilomar, January.

1994 Annual Alumni Conference in San Diego.

1995 Annual alumni Conference on Virtual Democracy at Lake Arrowhead, Southern California.

All Coro graduates are grateful to the dedicated group of graduates who saw this project through and who have made it possible for graduates from all over the country to have continuing association with each other and with Coro.

Earliest Attempts

CNAA was not the first attempt at an alumni association. An informal alumni organization existed from the beginning. Alumni regularly appeared at graduations, fund raisers, solicited donors, acted as mentors and interviewees. In November of 1966, the core Coro alumni supporters met at the Golden Tee Resort in Morro Bay for several days of program and renewal. A memorable "jam session" brought out the Aleshires with guitar and banjo, Jerry Jones on trumpet and Bob Coate on piano. Both W. Donald Fletcher and Van Dyne Dodge were there to inspire and challenge. Not enough organizational energy existed at that time for a formal organization to emerge, but those who were there then and gave it a try rejoice to see the prosperity of the present National Coro Alumni Association. About time!

CNAA Officers, 1989–1992

President,
 Ray Roeder
Vice President,
 Jack Fine
 Hong Van
 Diane Torres
Secretary, John Robinson
Treasurer, Harvey Charnofsky

Officers 1992–1993

Presidents,
 Mary Ellen Irwin
 John Robinson
Vice Presidents:
 Fran Aleshire, Southern California
 Mack Bradley, Midwest
 Cheryl Kerr Edwards, Northern California
 Tom Polk, New York
Secretary: Annette Conklin
Treasurer: Harvey Charnofsky

Officers 1994–1995

President,
 Ed Gerber
Vice Presidents:
 Jack D. Fine, Southern California
 Andrew Kimball, New York
 Mort Raphael, Northern California
 Mack Bradley, Midwest
Secretary: Annette Conklin
Treasurer: Laddie Hughes

Achievements

America is especially good at training experts, specialists and managers, but we are in special need of training multi-segment leaders: persons who have a global perspective and understanding that what once were tidy lines between domestic and international, public and private are irretrievably blurred.

Thomas E. Cronin

We must develop networks of leaders, drawn from all segments, who accept some measure of responsibility for the community's shared concerns. I call them networks of responsibility—leaders of disparate or conflicting interests who undertake to act collaboratively on behalf of the shared concerns of the community and the nation.

John Gardner

Imagine yourself trying to describe a tree to a person who had lived all of his life in a desert area totally bereft of any type of tree. What would you say? How could you describe the complexity of the structure, the marvel of adaptation, the intricacy of processes, the intimate relationship of tree to environment? If you tried your best, would the person ever have the "sense" of the tree?

How much more effective if you could just take the individual and lead him to a tree.

So it is that, ultimately, Coro needs to take you to meet its graduates. Here they are. Here is what they are doing. Here is what they care about. Here is what they say about their Coro experience. This chapter tries to do the next best thing to a personal encounter. Please, judge for yourself.

WHAT TO EXPECT FROM CORO GRADUATES
by Robert L. Coate SF '49

Robert Coate, now deceased, VP of Winfield and Company, was State Treasurer of the Democratic Party and the first Coro graduate to be appointed to the Coro Board of Trustees. He then became Chairman.

Long ago I learned not to analyze "What is Coro?" but to discuss Coro's graduates instead. These "products" answer the question better than any program description.

Talking to Coro graduates has been an intriguing and practical time saver for me. I do business with Washington agencies, and I have discovered how helpful it is to call Coro to find out if there is a graduate working in that agency. If so, I call this stranger, and in ten minutes I learn more than I might by going to Washington itself. With Coro graduates, I find it easy to get to the point and to understand the circumstances involved.

Coro people have an excellent sense of what America is all about. They realize that the complex interplay among government, business, labor and other institutions is in fact a system that has gone far beyond the past century's titles, labels and slogans. People who get important tasks done are usually impressed with a foundation which helps younger people feel affirmative about our complicated system.

After many years of puzzling over the steps effective people use to get hard jobs done, I have come up with an oversimplified answer. Sense, consensus, consent. First, an idea must make sense to the proponent. Second, he usually talks it through with friends and associates for whose judgment he has regard, or perhaps with individuals whose views are likely to vary widely. The point is to seek consensus. Third, he seeks the consent of large numbers of people.

We who make up these large numbers of people are called "voters" by politicians, the "masses" by yearny thinkers, the "uncommitted" by hopefuls, "markets" by businessmen, etc. Whatever we are, not very much of real importance in America will take place unless a lot of us consent. Almost no one is smart enough to take an idea that makes sense to him and get our consent without having established prior consensus.

On the other hand, we do not respond well to one who espouses a consensus unless it seems clear to us that it makes sense to him also. Coro graduates go through all three steps.

One other trait! Viet Nam and Mississippi nick at the Coro graduate. He is irked by people who rant at "politicians" but do nothing themselves. He assumes that the public sectors of our society are his personal responsibility. With the sense of common purpose, with accumulated experience and knowledge, any number of Coro graduates could be a worthwhile and impressive public force.

IT'S TOUGH TO PLAY IN THE MIDDLE
by Mike Roos

Mike Roos, former Democratic Majority Leader in the California Assembly was Executive Director of the Los Angeles Coro offices in the early '70s.
Coro gave me my basic approach to getting things done when I went to the Assembly. I went in believing that it is the people who play in the middle who basically move the process forward, so that's where I wanted to be. What I didn't know was how tough it is to be in that position where sometimes you feel like you have no friends at all. You have to put together coalitions to get votes, so I learned to suspend my beliefs so I could listen to someone else's position. When I succeeded, I usually could find some way to move, some position that satisfied us both.

What's tough is that the press and often the public think you have no principles. You want to be a purist like everyone else, but you can't because, that way, nothing moves.

For example, getting consensus on the gun bill was really hard. I had to listen to one guy pontificate for hours about the 4th Amendment. Finally I said, "Forget the bill, just tell me what you could vote for." He gave me his background, a feel for his values, and I found I could pull out some things in the legislation he could go along with. The essence of the bill was preserved, and he voted for it. That's the Coro approach.

Coro gives you enough listening time with labor, with business, with government people, with special interests, so you can pretty much predict how they are going to go. This is a great viewing platform for a legislator. When you find someone who can see through multiple lenses, accomodate multiple belief systems and still move the process along, that's rare. That's what is needed. Coro is one of the few training programs which systematically produces this kind of talent.

COMMUNITY VOUCHES FOR CORO

In 1958 Ford Foundation awarded Coro a grant which permitted a major expansion of the program to Los Angeles. After only ten years of operation, Coro had earned the confidence of persons of influence who were willing to vouch for the program's integrity and effectiveness. Who were these people? What did they say?

"We have found that interns upon completing their Internship have gone out into the fields of business, industry and government with goodwill toward the labor movement. We believe that labor should cooperate with this organization."

Daniel Del Carlo,
Building/Construction Trades Council, S.F.

"It is imperative that we have individuals of quality, properly trained for direct and indirect public careers. Civic leaders . . . are both pleased and impressed with Coro's record . . . the policies of the Coro Foundation have proven themselves on a small scale and warrant your support so they can expand their work."

Jean Witter,
Dean Witter & Co.

"Coro Foundation, within its limited budget, has in the short time of its operation contributed outstandingly in getting young men and women of the highest character and ability into government work."

Preston Hotchkis,
Founders' Fire & Marine Insurance

"Because of its original approach to some of the most difficult problems of our times and the very practical method which Coro has devised as to their solution, I have maintained my interest. Coro deserves support."

John E. Cushing,
Matson Navigation

"We have had in our office at the Chronicle a number of Coro interns who have been very efficient and I am glad to say of a mental attitude that is quite satisfactory. We think Coro should be encouraged in their work."

George Cameron,
San Francisco Chronicle

"My observation leads me to believe that Coro Foundation is performing an outstandingly worthwhile service in the area of public affairs."

T.A. Brooks,
Chief Administrative Officer, San Francisco

"Based upon my personal observation and comments made by my colleagues...that no finer contribution to our municipality's governmental development could be made than is being accomplished by Coro Foundation."

Chester R. MacPhee,
Chairman Bd/Supervisors, S.F.

Just a small sample!

ACHIEVEMENTS AND TESTIMONIES

Coro has matured from an early social and political experiment to a valued national asset.

San Francisco Chronicle

In this era, many Americans have found it easier to turn off rather than turn on. Coro interns have chosen involvement rather than alienation. Our association with Coro goes back over many years. Coro has given us more than we have given it.

Otis Chandler, Los Angeles Times

WHAT DO CORO GRADUATES DO?

We offer a sampling of what Coro graduates do. The sample is taken from New York. Here are some of the positions and activities of graduates of the New York Fellows program. One individual was trained at another Center but is living in New York.

Anne Bailey
Executive Director,
The Albert G. Oliver Program

Vivian Vasquez
Director,
Citizen's Advice Bureau

Sarah Williams
Manager,
Pfizer Education Initiative

Andrew Kimball
Assistant to the President,
New York Public Library

Andrew Rubinson
Director,
Fresh Youth Initiatives

John Miottel
Program Officer,
Fund for NYC Public Education

Timothy Tompkins
Special Assistant to President,
NYC Economic Development Corp

Victoria Wong
Public Policy Coordinator,
Asian Americans for Equality

Quentin Spector
Executive Director,
Municipal Assistance Corp.

Dirk Smillie
Executive Assistant,
Freedom Forum Media Studies Center

The Coro Alumni Directory is a listing of persons active in all spheres of community life. But what they signal in common is a keen interest in how public policy issues are developing, a desire to be in the midst of citizen initiatives, to be fully participative and engaged.

Whatever Coro does and however it does it, the evidence is conclusive that the training produces productive, positive and active citizens and leaders.

Our society needs good people at all levels of government, involved in all aspects of civic life. Monsanto backs Coro because this program is one of significance in America today.

John W. Hanley,
Chairman of the Board, Monsanto Company

If we are to emerge from the present situation, inwhich any organization larger or more complex than a neighborhood bowling league is viewed on all sides with suspicion and thereforehampered in its ability to perform, it will only be by educating a much larger proportion of our people in what it takes to make organizations run, and in what can and cannot, fairly be expected of them by the public they serve. Coro helps in a most direct and practical way to achieve that . . .

A hundred Coro Foundations across the country would not be too many.

Richard Lyman,
President, Rockefeller Foundation;
former President, Stanford University

Coro and its work mean there will be a core of anxious and dedicated people entering community life with a unique and rigorous background. I've seen their dedication first hand. They give unselfishly of themselves. Their commitment is total.

Lloyd McBride, President,
United Steel Workers of America

Our commitment to Coro stems from the fact that this organization is truly fulfilling a most important need. Coro's program is, in my opinion, one of the most successful public service efforts anywhere.

Thornton Bradshaw,
CEO, RCA, former president Atlantic Richfield

COMMENTS FROM CORO FELLOWS

Five years ago, I walked into a disenfranchised community with a lot of walking wounded and a lot of single adults looking for alternative life styles. With luck and hard work, I created half a dozen social service agencies. I don't think I could have done that without a sense of how government operates.

Rev. James Conn,
the Church in Ocean Park, SF, '69

One of my most vivid memories of Coro is trekking through long dark hallways in San Francisco's Chinatown sweatshops with a union agent—a memory that has returned as I write about labor. Reality wasn't neat theories, but complex economic and human relationships. It's an invaluable experience for a journalist—or anyone else.

Helen Dewar, Reporter,
Washington Post & Times Herald, SF, '58

WESTERN UNION TELEGRAM

LC500 ODG65
O UA344 GOVT PD THE WHITE HOUSE WASHINGTON DC 11 757P EDT=
M DONALD FLETCHER, CARE ASST HOTEL MGR ON DUTY,
VAN DUYN A DODGE=
CORO FOUNDATION TESTIMONIAL DINNER AMBASSADOR HOTEL
LOSA=
I WANT TO EXTEND MY VERY BEST WISHES ON THE OCCASION OF
THE CORO ALUMNI ASSOCIATION'S TESTIMONIAL BANQUET. THE
CORO FOUNDATION HAS ESTABLISHED A DISTINGUISHED RECORD
S ETCHING ACROSS ALMOST TWO DECADES IN PREPARING MEN
AND WOMEN FOR EFFECTIVE PARTICIPATION IN PUBLIC AFFAIRS.
THE ROSTER OF YOUR GRADUATES, AND PARTICULARLY YOUR
DISTINGUISHED GUEST SPEAKER, ELIZABETH SMITH, IS A VERY
REAL TRIBUTE TO THE SUCCESS OF YOUR EFFORTS. IN THIS TIME
OF UNPARALLELED NEED AND OPPORTUNITY FOR PUBLIC LEADERSHIP
OF THE HIGHEST CALIBER, AND FOR NEW MEANS TO REALIZE THE
FULL POTENTIAL OF OUR FREE SOCIETY, THE WORK OF THE CORO
FOUNDATION TAKES ON SPECIAL SIGNIFICANCE.
I AM GLAD TO HAVE THE OPPORTUNITY TO EXPRESS MY
APPRECIATION TO YOU FOR YOUR IMAGINATION AND DEDICATION
DEVELOPING AND SUSTAINING THIS PROGRAM=
JOHN F KENNEDY.

My Coro training led me directly into a leadership role in foundation-funded community and statewide tutorial projects in Los Angeles and North Carolina. Several of the projects I started in the mid-60's are still going strong.

Lowell Dodge, Assoc. Dir.
Economic & Area Dev. U.S. General Accounting Office
LA, '64

Coro enhanced my sensitivity to people and helped me to better fathom their needs and concerns. I learned to bring objectivity to the political system. This training has stood me in good stead in working for many candidates over the years. While the socioeconomic backdrop has changed, the fundamental lessons learned through Coro remain sound in every setting. In essence, Coro gave me the confidence to work with a variety of human beings. I've discovered that ability is more difficult to attain than mastery of subject matter.

Vic Fazio, U.S. Congressman,
Calif., LA, '66

My training as a Coro Fellow, with its emphasis on real world experiences, has been invaluable in providing me with the skills necessary to work closely with all segments of the community to develop efficient, effective and responsible programs that affect the lives of thousands of citizens.

Michael Giger, Ass't Dir Research/Dev,
St. Louis County Dept of Human Resources, SL, '73

Coro was one of the most influential experiences of my life. It absolutely convinced me to pursue a career in public service.

Dianne Feinstein, Mayor of SF,
U.S. Senator, California, SF, '56

That one year in Coro had more impact on my life than anything else I've ever done. The sixties were a time in which we tended to divide people up into simple categories: good guys and bad guys. I spent a year interviewing "bad guys" who were delightful. The experience opened me up to the fact that people who approached things differently from myself could have equally valid reasons.

John Greenwood,
Member LA School Board, Realtor, LA, '68

THE WHITE HOUSE
WASHINGTON

AUGUST 5, 1982

I welcome this 40th anniversary of the Coro Foundation as an occasion to express my continuing high regard for the "Mission of Coro."

For 40 years, the Coro Foundation has worked to build leaders. In reaching out to individuals with the potential for leadership and growth and by helping them to gain firsthand experience and expertise in a wide range of public service areas, Coro has helped shape America's future.

Coro fellowships granted to talented men and women, which are combined with nine months of full-time experience-based training, provide an invaluable opportunity for leadership preparation. The Coro Foundation must take great pride in its record of success. Today Coro graduates can be found in responsible positions at all levels of business and government and in community service throughout America. I commend the Coro Foundation, its graduates, and its supporters for their commitment to excellence and for their spirit of innovation and initiative.

As we face the challenges of an ever-changing and increasingly complex world, Coro will continue to play a vital role in training leaders of tomorrow.

You have my heartfelt congratulations and my every best wish on this 40th anniversary.

Ronald Reagan

The Coro Internship provides a golden educational opportunity for training in the field of public affairs. I personally credit Coro for whatever business success I had, showing me where the doors to opportunity lay open, and crystallizing my commitment to public service. There is a huge gap between the ivory tower of a political science classroom and the real world of politics and government. Coro plays a key role in efforts to bridge this gap.

**Jerry Lewis, US Congressman,
California, LA, '57**

I've found that the Coro background and training opens doors that might be harder to open because of partisanship. There is immediate acceptance because of Coro training. Coro graduates appear to be more open to other points of view, rather than being locked in by partisan tunnel-vision.

**Donald Livingston, VP,
Carter Hawley Hale Stores, LA, '61**

The Coro Foundation does not have a monopoly on teaching leadership skills. Military organizations, police departments, political, business and labor groups all have programs. But, so far as I am aware, Coro and LC are the only organizations which have no political agenda. They strive to empower individuals, trusting that they will make our system function better. I received a gift from Coro, the gift of an attitude. At no time since then have I felt a victim. When I wanted influence, I knew I could have it. This is a gift of incredible value.

**Alan E. Ellis,
Judge of the Justice Court, Idaho, LA, '67**

I remember Selection Day vividly. It was the most challenging, exhausting and thrilling day of my life. Since then Coro has always been a part of my life. I've served on selection boards, the LA Board and now the National Board. Of all the many organizations I associate with, Coro is clearly the closest to my heart. It's partly the friendships, partly the trust you gain in Coro associates. If I have fifty calls on my desk, I ring back the Coro people first. Coro people interrelate and bring projects to pass in many unpredictable ways over a lifetime.

**Bruce Corwin, President
Metropolitan Theaters Corp., LA, '63,
Chairman of the Coro National Board of Directors.**

HOW DOES CORO TRAINING CHANGE THE INDIVIDUAL?

by Donald Ehrman, Ph.D.

Don Fletcher once asked a trained observer to comment on the changes he witnessed in Fellows over the period of their internship. No one has ever said it better than Donald Ehrman, Ph.D., a leading Bay Area psychologist, who responded this way:

Confidence

The newly selected Fellow seems young. He sometimes seems cautious; sometimes overly-assertive; rarely at ease with his opinions. He tends often to be insecurely competitive, or tending to withdraw from interchange. He seems overly focused on achievement and on proving himself. He often plays a role which does not seem fully integrated into him, so that one can get a feeling in talking with him of being responded to as a symbol rather than as an individual. Actually, he seems "wet behind the ears" and fearful that his inadequacy will be exposed. One of the interesting things in the Coro training program is how it originally stimulates this feeling, operating to make the Fellow even more insecure, yet generally without the Fellow suffering basic loss of self-esteem.

When the Fellow graduates, he seems to me somewhat brash. He has learned to look for the gimmick, and he may feel some contempt for the less sophisticated. But when you meet him several months later, that brashness has worn off. Instead, he gives a feeling of sureness and a willingness to operate in a multifaceted world which suggests a process continuing after graduation toward constructive maturation. This is what I mean by the sense of confidence which I feel the Fellow experiences. He has gained confidence in his power and ability to operate toward goals.

Ability to listen

Originally, the young Coro selectee seems mainly oriented toward demonstration of his own skills and knowledge. He wants to have, and to give, THE ANSWER. Discussion is argumentation, and the important thing is to convince the other party. The graduated Fellow has the capacity to listen and a real interest in finding out what the other person thinks. He wants to find value in the other person's thoughts. He does not give the impression of someone who is without opinions of his own, but he does give the impression that he is able to tolerate differences from those opinions and to modify those he holds. He seems able to express himself in a manner and at a time which encourages others to listen to him and weigh his words rather than provoking controversy. I think that this asset results from his learning to listen. His expression of his own thoughts is more probably going to be in tune with the other person's readiness to hear than it would if his self expression were essentially divorced from the interpersonal context in which he finds himself.

Conceptual flexibilty

I think this flexibility originally manifests in a somewhat unconstructive form: the tendency to look for the gimmick in all human behavior. But this is the tendency of those who, on learning a new skill, wish to use it more than is necessary for the pleasure of achievement. The more constructive result, and the longer-lasting one, comes in the readiness of the graduated Coro Fellow to try to integrate materials from different contexts, to seek connections between apparently differing truths, to challenge the obvious without dismissing it, to welcome the novel without too hastily embracing it, and to see the multiplicity of paths to any goal. This is a difficult quality to describe meaningfully without example; but I think your more successful graduates have learned to be skeptical without being cynical, and receptive without being credulous.

Development of a group identity

I sense a strong attachment to the Coro group which the Fellow develops during training. Through this attachment, an individual can develop ideals of public service and standards of public behaviour which can be potent forces in guiding his future career. They stand as unverbalized "givens" of the atmosphere. In this period of our culture, when group identifications seem to be replacing to some extent the sense of rightness and worth based formerly in a sense of individual "belonging", there are many aspects of affiliation with a group that are frightening. The conformity demanded by the Coro group, however, seems to differ from the many conformities in avoiding stereotyping of thought and behavior. It seems to demand only that action be guided by principle and that others' attitudes and beliefs be respected.

These, then, are the end results of Coro training which leap to mind. I can think of specific experiences I have had to confirm the statements I make. You've had your failures, no doubt, but your batting average is impressively high. You seem to me to be accomplishing all that education should accomplish, but what our present system often fails to accomplish even with its most gifted prospects.

Visions of the Future

Life is not a problem to be solved but a mystery to be lived.

Yeats

We end this Coro collection by returning to the vision of W.D. Fletcher and asking him what unfinished tasks he sees for Coro and for his companion program, Liaison Citizens.

WDF LETTER TO CORO FELLOWS

In 1991, he wrote a letter to the graduating class of Coro Fellows in which he spoke to them in a personal way about how they could build on their Coro experience. He speaks to all Coro graduates as follows:

You are leaving Coro now, and I would ask that you consider yourselves as trustees for Coro's future, especially as Coro and its graduates have a privileged role in our society. All phases of society have accepted you and offered insight into their valued fields. Judging by example of past Coro graduates, you will do well in whatever field you choose, and you will contribute to those fields. But I ask more of you as trustees for Coro's future.

Americans are an independent people, coming from the old countries to make their way in new surroundings, and today, individualism, is the key theme. Each person and institution seeks self-sufficiency; and because of diversity of interests, conflict is often the rule, a competition among groups to secure their share (or more). Government as an arbitrator is being overwhelmed with that

responsibility, that of watching out for the interests of all, and tryng to cope with ever more complex problems.

Coro and its graduates have a larger role—that of providing a new viewpoint for the American people—of seeking ways to serve society as a whole, and this is primarily a political and spiritual challenge. It is being capable of *refusing conflict and of creating common means of solving differences*—and not going to some institution or government agency. It is being committed to seeking and enhancing the spiritual qualities of society.

Perhaps these words have little meaning for you now. Thus I have a suggestion. In your everyday encounters, seek to understand *the ongoing politics of your involvement and how you and other parties can enable those political involvements to have quality and integrity.* This will be a matter of discovery on your part for no textbook or series of editorials can provide the requisite insights.

I suggest that spiritual meanings surround people and institutions with even more impact than economic, social and political meanings combined. This statement may also not communicate. I know, however, that spiritual meanings are ever present—and simply require identifying on your part.

I suggest an approach as old as humanity. Go looking, interpret what you find, conceptualize whether your interpretation relates to the political or spiritual field. Above all, don't hide your discoveries but always obtain insight and interpretations from others and thus create a wholesome way of relating to the political and spiritual fields. This immersion of effort was followed by Van Duyn Dodge, our Coro associates and myself from the beginning -pre-Coro, January, 1941.

You will be rewarded. You will develop a fascination for your searching/interpreting. You will suddenly find life has more quality and freshness. You will more likely look for the good points in others, and you will stimulate character building in institutions. The larger numbers of Coro graduates so involved will bring about the potential of a "critical mass" which will enable our society to become more of a Great Community—which John Dewey emphasized 70 years ago and whose thinking was offered to many Coro training groups.

This is just a dream, perhaps, but dreams can have larger than life impact, bypassing the status quo.

Fletcher also saw new tasks for the institutions of Coro and Liaison Citizens. He saw that although great progress had been made through many years of experimentation in orientation and training of participants, the research elements of the programs had suffered neglect. The constant stresses of recruiting, staging and organizing programs and the press of fund-raising had diminished the time and energy that could be directed to evaluating and researching the conceptual accuracy of the programs and evaluating results. Also, profound changes in society had occurred which needed to be factored into this research.

WDF LETTER TO FRIENDS

In a letter to friends dated October, 1992, Fletcher wrote the following:

Always the political power of society is in the people, and always society is seeking to manipulate and harness that power—usually for specific ends and benefits to given groups. Never in history have people been enabled to direct their innate political power from a sound knowledge base.

This is inexpressibly sad. History shows the terrible toll paid because of society's failure, not because of people's failure. People's instruments of governing do not allow people to truly govern themselves.

LC's thinking preceded Coro's but was terminated in 1945 because of failure to secure funding. Coro's thinking never fully acquired the knowledge base which was created from 1941–45. I believe the time is ripe to have these two institutions undertake a joint research project which would produce solid data indicating how people can learn how to create effective self-governing orientation and discipline. Once data and interpretations re: citizen involvement in governing political processes are produced, we can take the necessary steps to develop intellectual structure useful for each institution.

Coro takes the "high road" and trains for administration, decison making and policy development while LC takes the "low road" and orients people for citizen-community involvement, in their offices, schools, playgrounds, and community at large.

In these two papers, Fletcher sets out a strong vision of the future and a mission to be accomplished by Coro graduates, both as individuals and by enlarging the purpose of the institutions he founded. The founders were inspired by far more than a desire to produce more dedicated and competent leaders for our society; they discerned the urgent need to get on with creating the Great Community spoken of by John Dewey. "A vast intelligence lies all around us," wrote that seer, "but it cannot be utilized for our common benefit while it remains inchoate and unexpressed. Individuals will develop that potential and find their true purpose when they can link up with their human companions and become trustees for the institutions they create and for this nurturing planet in whose beneficence we all share."

What steps could be taken by Coro and LC? Means must be found for graduates to come together and re-evaluate their training, to factor in their experiences out in the world and to think deeply about the current status of society. This might be done in conjunction with an Institute to Train Trainers. Such an institute would bring former trainers and advanced graduates together for a concentrated period of time. They could scope the mission and initiate plans to design the program and to secure funding.

We live in a time of deep soul-searching in America. Many discern that the fragmentation of the body politic has progressed so far that the center is in danger of not holding. Loyalty to America as a whole is rarely expressed by many minority groups; many youth find their education unfocused and without meaning to them, and increased criminal activity informs us that the "left out" among us are full of rage.

On the other hand, fresh thinking is taking place. The reorientation of science through quantum theory is altering our view of reality fundamentally. Community leadership programs are springing up in cities all across our nation, and citizens are actively volunteering to cope with social problems. New foundations are funding promising efforts to link citizens with their communities. Surely funding can be found to fulfill the dream of the Coro founders. This dream has demonstrated substance by reason of a fifty year history and the training of thousands of talented people who are already hard at work proving by the example of their lives that the dream is real and achievable.

Some Ending Thoughts

Reviewing the political atmosphere that led Dodge and Fletcher to launch the experiment that became Coro, an atmosphere in which various groups expressed their feelings of disenchantment with their society and their alienation from government, and then comparing that time to this period of similar hostility, we are tempted to conclude that the more things change, the more they stay the same. What has society learned in the last fifty years? What difference has Coro made?

One of the difficulties Coro has always encountered is the demand from funders and others that the answers to the above questions be delivered in a quantitative, results oriented frame of reference. But reality does not produce such neat categories. We shall probably never come to a juncture where we can say, "This society is healthy." "This society now understands what it is about." Coro has improved the leadership in this nation by 5%" etc. We deceive ourselves by trying to answer in a mode so unsuited to the essential mystery of human activity. Our ability to know is as obscure as that which we seek to know. Life is more a quest than a destination, and the impulse to seek answers is more life-giving than packaged answers.

Better questions are: "Do we have a good learning process going, and is there a means of adapting to what we are learning?" Pose these questions, and Coro can clearly document its progress and its contribution to our society.

Always the political power of society is in the people, and always society is seeking to manipulate and harness that power — usually for specific ends and benefits to given groups. Never in history have people been enabled to direct their innate political power from a sound knowledge base.

W. Donald Fletcher

There is a cumulative, powerful and irresistible effect flowing from the intelligent, well intentioned efforts of men and women striving to create a good and a just society. Recruiting and directing talented people into the flow of events where they can participate directly in this flow is perhaps the very most that can be done.

The insight that Dodge and Fletcher had, which was so unusual in the '40s, is that a universal political intelligence exists in the diverse elements of our society, the lowly as well as in those more favored by circumstance. This intelligence is there to be mobilized. What is missing is the connective tissue and a formulated intellectual base which would teach us how to form that tissue. What also continues to be missing are the occasions and the strategies which would give the separate elements the ability to form a greater unity. The intellectual discipline, the opportunities and the stategies are what Coro trained people might provide.

Another core insight the founders had was that the citizens appear to be those not invited to the party, indeed, they conceive of themselves this way. But it is the citizens who have the general attitude which can build the necessary bridges among groups. Coro has proved over fifty years that citizens, of all ages and circumstances, can be awakened, energized and mobilized to take active, positive roles in their communities and that, so mobilized and trained, they can provide the connective tissue and become the mediating influence needed by society.

If a man advances confidently in the direction of his dreams to live the life he has imagined, he will meet with a success unexpected in common hours.

Henry David Thoreau

field is to do a great deal, indeed. If we were to document all that Coro has accomplished and continues to accomplish, we would have to pry into the lives of all those touched by it and then calculate the consequences of their touching others and their impact upon the field of public policy where they have played—an impossible task.

This we know. Coro pioneered the idea of setting up internships to send students out to learn about public policy making first-hand. It remains the only internship program to include exposure to all elements of the community: business, labor, government, media, social services, the volunteer and non-proft sectors and others. It remains the only internship program to develop in participants a disciplined mode of observation and analysis. As far as we know, it is the only program to devise systematic training strategies and methodologies which can be replicated and which produce consistent results. The intellectual base is consistent with the most advanced theories of information, learning and relationships. Finally, with all of this, Coro has also produced a graduate network of thousands who are active leaders in their communities. Coro continues to project a promising and hopeful idea of how this democratic society can fulfill its promises. To those weighed down by discouragement over the performance of our leaders, Coro offers both solace and opportunity. Beginning with nothing but ideas and human energy, Coro affected the balance, changed the equation. All who know of Coro can rededicate themselves and do likewise. Indeed, why not?

CONCLUSION

In the arena of human affairs, no grand denouement can be expected. But in the working out of our life as a community, we are not so much children running around putting our fingers in the new holes which continue to appear in the dikes as we are players in a quantum field of ever changing events. To be a knowledgeable, willing and well-intentioned player in this

Fran Aleshire, Ed.D, editor of this collection, has a long time association with Coro. She was engaged to Frank Aleshire when he was going through the 1948 Fellows program, and she gained rare insight during the succeeding three years when Frank was a member of the early staff. During those years, staff and families frequently were invited to the Fletchers' Atherton home, and spouses were initiated into the Fletcher educational style and dramatizations. She attended General Semantics classes and social gatherings of those times. Later, in the 1950's, Fran was the trainer for several laboratory courses. In 1975, she was head trainer for a summer Internship for Wellesley women in Los Angeles. In 1982, she and Frank did a comprehensive evaluation of the Liaison Citizens Program. Shortly thereafter, Don Fletcher invited Fran to write a training manual for that program. In preparation, Fran spent many days observing the program and consulting with WDF. Then, in 1988, Fran and Frank were invited to evaluate the Coro program in St. Louis. Again she had many opportunities to interview participants, staff and board members. Finally, Fran was asked by the National Board of Governors to interview representative staff and produce national program standards for Coro. This task completed, the National Board adopted these standards in 1989.

Fran became an early participant and supporter of the Coro National Alumni Association. Her frequent contacts with graduates, her visits to Center offices, her writing skills and her long time association with W. D. Fletcher made her an obvious choice to edit this volume for the Alumni Association.

Professionally, Fran has worked as high school teacher and administrator. She earned her BA from Stanford University, her MA from Whittier College and her Ed.D. from Arizona State University. Her dissertation was on the subject of communication between school boards and superintendents, and this led to consulting with school systems and cities, building trust/communication between elected officials and administrative staff.

Fran is currently founder, trainer and program director of a community leadership program in North San Diego County, following the Coro model.

Digital typefaces used are Koch Antiqua, Stone Sans and
Adobe Garamond from Adobe Systems.

 Graphic design by David Sibbet
The Grove Consultants International
San Francisco, California

Typographical design and
production management by Paul Benkman
Tiki Bob Publishing & Design
San Francisco, California

Digital Graphics by Robert L. Pardini
Production Assistance by Thomas Sibbet
The Grove Consultants International